The Parent Playbook

Proven Strategies for Guiding
Your Child to Thrive in the K-12 Education System

DR. CASSANDRA HARRIS

CONTENTS

PREFACE

In the following pages, the word *student* is used interchangeably in the context of a school classroom and in the context of your home. These references are on purpose. It is intended to remind us, as parents, that we are our children's most significant teachers. Even when we think they are not watching or listening, they are. They are truly sponges, absorbing most of what they see and hear. In our homes, children begin to develop a filter that will either siphon away what is not good or should not be normal for their lives or funnel those things into their lives, which become who they are. Matthew 18:18 tells us that "whatever [we] bind on earth will be bound in heaven, and whatever [we] loose on earth will be loosed in heaven." I believe this to be true with our children as well. Whatever ideals, whatever visions, whatever dreams, and whatever shortcomings parents have, it can be released into the lives of our children through our words *and* our actions. This is why so many parents can recognize the good in their children. It is also why some children, even into adulthood, blame their parents for the negative characteristics and experiences they received from their home lives.

Up to the age of 5-6, children's brains are being developed more than at any other time in their lives.[1] During this time, their environments are crucial in shaping their beliefs. To be specific, the existence of a poor

---

1   Lenroot and Giedd, (2006).

physical environment, meaning void of financial wealth, certainly does not mean that a poor child will develop. It is important for parents to know that family economic status does not have to be the most influential factor in a child's future success. I believe that words spoken and heard profoundly influence what children think they can do, see, and defeat. As in any case, there are exceptions. My charge for all parents, as imperfect as we are, is to know that children are a gift from God. It was not intended that our lives be perfect before we receive them, but it is purposed that the perfect one within us would be allowed to flow through our beings to produce humans with the same or more promise. In Psalms 115: 14-15, the word says, "The Lord will increase [us] more and more, you and your children." In our shortcomings, we must remember that they become more of what they see than what they hear. When we fall, it is crucial to be the example of quick apology and mending because it teaches them how to own wrongdoing, recover from it, avoid reoccurrence, and, more importantly, forgive. It also teaches them to develop that funnel of good or bad within their own lives that may not be what they saw but what they learned to be that is best for them through trial and error and gentle guidance within their home experiences. More importantly, it is vital to be their 'stoves' and not have them to touch danger or error to recognize or discern it. Instead, hear your ways to avoid life's potholes and continue to climb and thrive in their journey. Let us continue to celebrate their growth and the queens and kings who are obedient enough to God to want more for their children!

ACKNOWLEDGEMENTS

In my son, Ryan, I see so much of God. I see Him in my son's adventurous and fearless spirit, in his confidence, and in his love for people. He has supported me in many projects, and this one was no different. As he grows into adulthood, I am so thankful to have had the privilege of parenting him. I want to thank him for being an amazing son and for prompting the writing of this book. May God bless him always, and may he always remember, with fondness, our bond.

-Mom

Cheree Wiley, CEO of Diverse Perspectives (www.dpdei.com) – My sister in Christ, I thank you for your professional guidance in bringing this book into being. What a blessing it is that God saw fit to connect us in this effort. Thank you for everything!

Dr. Titinesha Llewellyn - There are no words for the value I place on our friendship. Thank you for your "eagle-eye" review, feedback, and investment in me. Friends for life.

Acknowledgements

CHAPTER 1

UNDERSTANDING THE K12 EDUCATION SYSTEM AN OVERVIEW

There has been a widening gap between school systems and parents for far too long. One of the primary disconnects is found in the complexity of the school system. For those who have been a part of a school system and a few who have not, it is widely known that the many moving parts of a school system demand a management style highly comparable to a business with its own language and processes. Unfortunately, only some outside of the educational system have an opportunity to learn the language of school. In this context, language is not only the words spoken or definitions known within school walls but also the known impact that one topic area or subject has on another from year to year.

While none of this information is a secret, not having access to what happens in a school system routinely presents somewhat of a blind spot to busy parents and families. For educated and uneducated parents, clearing this blind spot can present an opportunity to bridge gaps so that language flows fluently and frequently between parents and schools. This book is written by a parent who spent over 10 years in the K12 system while parenting a young child. During that time, I marveled at the number of things I did not know about how a school system worked early on. As I learned new things from year to year, I wondered how parents who did not know the school system could ever navigate such a complex system and gain all its benefits; without their knowing the many things I learned while working in education.

Within these pages, I hope you find practical ways to help advocate for your child and partner with your school's system to help your student become more successful and feel more loved. Schools can feel isolating and overwhelming to students without partnership at home and school. As you begin to evolve in your understanding of the language of schools, please be patient with your partners, teachers, and principals. Invite them into your world as you enter theirs. Together (parents, teachers, school districts), students benefit and thrive in our collective support. Divided, students suffer and are alone, isolated, and discouraged. As parents, together with the education system, we gain so much by bridging the communication gap between us. I hope that each chapter within "The Parent Playbook: Proven Strategies for Guiding Your Child to Thrive in the K-12 Education System" increases your K12 language prowess and your passion for partnering with your child and the school system toward their social and academic success.

CHAPTER 2

THE SILENT ROBBER HOW ABSENTEEISM DIRECTLY IMPACTS LEARNING

Many discussion topics surround public school attendance and its impact on student achievement and well-being. One of the more powerful but practical actions for parents is ensuring their children regularly attend school and are in the classroom as scheduled. Achieving this may sound easy enough, but undoubtedly, unassuming factors can influence the number of days children are in school and in the proper room at the required time. For this chapter's discussion, an absence is considered any school day a student is not in their expected classroom when school is open for student attendance.

ACADEMIC IMPACT

When students are absent, the overall impact on them is thought to be far-reaching. Student absences have been associated with lower test scores and grades, behavioral issues, and higher dropout incidents.[2] With some of the more prioritized goals, such as earning passing test scores and grades at stake, the contributors to absenteeism are worthy of deeper understanding to recognize causes and prevent them. To believe that only chronic incidents of absences have an impact would be to miss the fact that even small absences can have an enormous impact on student's lives.[3] Studies also suggest that students with a family history of parents or siblings struggling to provide academic help to catch up when they fall behind due to missed classes are more likely to repeat grades and ultimately drop out of school.[4]

There is an analogy that makes the impact of days out of school clearer. Middle and high school students generally see five to seven teachers each day. Each teacher may have 20 to 30 students, and one teacher could teach more than 150 students daily! How powerful it is when we think about how little time teachers have to spend with children who are not on pace due to chronic absenteeism to help them regain academic ground. Of course, the potential losses associated with absenteeism do not stop at academic impact; other adverse effects are also associated with student absences. For instance, chronic absenteeism also threatens a child's emotional connection with themselves and others.

---

2   Gershenson, et al., (2017); Gottfried, (2010, 2011); Gottfried and Kirksey, (2017); U.S. Department of Education, (2019).
3   Kirksey, (2019); Klein et al., (2022).
4   Chang & Romero, (2008); Ready, (2010).

SOCIAL ABSENCE IMPACT

When children chronically miss days in school, they also miss the opportunity to interact with their peers. Especially during their younger years, PreK-5th grade, children are vastly developing, and the very foundations for their ability to socialize and interact with others are being formed.[5] Students who are under-socialized because they miss the opportunity to coexist with children their age consistently can feel isolated and perhaps even awkward, contributing to a spiraling cycle of adverse effects within their personal and academic lives. If the child is kept out of school and does not develop social skills, once that child does come into the school building, there is a high possibility that the child will not want to be there. This can happen due to a lack of peer relationships and not feeling part of the school culture. Similarly, chronic absenteeism can make developing friendships harder; as a result, such children can think that they have no support system at school, creating feelings of isolation and loneliness. Finally, whether the impact is a loss of social attachment or academic loss, each can be avoided by identifying and making efforts to circumvent known causes of absenteeism.

CAUSES OF ABSENTEEISM

A. LOW PARENT INVOLVEMENT

Students, no matter their age, sense the expectations of their parents. Given a child's early need to feel accepted by their parents, children often look for queues from their parents to support their positive beliefs in themselves.[6] Most parents enter their children into school with very high hopes and expectations. Unfortunately, if a child is not reading by third grade, when the expectation for them to do so increases,

---

5   Finn, (1989); Heckman et al., (2006); Korpershoek, et al., (2020).
6   Cheung and Pomerantz, (2012); Sheldon, (2009).

some parents feel defeated and lose what were once high hopes for their child's academic progress. It is so important that children know parents believe in their ability to excel and secure desirable futures, even when their academic performance waivers a bit. Students must have a "cheerleader" at home that they can depend on to provide them with words of encouragement and a show of faith that their life and academic success are possible. Studies suggest that students are 6x more likely to try harder and are less likely to give up in school and classes if the parents exhibit behaviors that suggest they believe in their child's ability to achieve and their capability to push through obstacles to excel in their academic lives.[7] Parents demonstrating that they are steadfast in their belief of their child's future may occasionally mean believing in their students beyond what may appear contrary at the moment while showing their children their faith in their ability to prevail. Parents must continue to believe in their students even if what they see is not what they want to see yet. Students need to know that although they struggle in an area, it does not mean they cannot achieve.

STORY TIME - MY OWN LESSONS LEARNED (CONSISTENT INVOLVEMENT HAS IMPACT)

Consistent parental involvement can be very impactful in ensuring that students stay within proper progress levels and know that they have an advocate at home and in school.

I remember when my son started kindergarten. I entered that space believing we were (because I was married then) investing in a private school experience. I expected this meant engaged teachers who were leading in the classroom and would need or want little assistance from parents. Furthermore, I really believed I was paying for an expert, and that expert would engage me as needed. My way of thinking couldn't have been further from the

---

7   Bogenschneider, (1997).

truth. Within days of starting in the private kindergarten, I quickly noticed a somewhat casually conveyed but albeit troubling feedback from the teacher's assistant. I discovered that the teacher had "tagged" my son as somewhat behind because he did not know some of the concepts she explained would have been introduced while in *PreK* had he attended. I thought PreK was optional, but I'll focus more on that later. As a parent, routinely asking questions of your student's teachers is critical to your student's success. In fact, it's vital.

Had I not been actively involved in monitoring and continuously asking questions, my son would have been looked over, under-taught, and possibly more susceptible to falling behind in his early academic years. I was determined that my son would not be labeled because he had not gone to PreK. My highest focus was to uncover what my child didn't know so that I could fill the gaps with the information my son was missing. During this time, I saw my vivacious son begin to be much quieter when I picked him up and not as enthusiastic about going to school, whereas prior, he was so excited to meet his new school friends. During this time, I saw a complete change in my son's energy and enthusiasm about attending school. Once I could work with his teacher and school, showing an active interest, I could help him make a turnaround in his academics. The response from both my son and his school was like night and day when I became more involved in the process.

The key to partnering with my son's teacher in kindergarten was my beginning to engage in more in-depth and routine questions. I must also add that I was uncomfortable talking with the teacher because I did not want to be perceived as confrontational. Looking back, I was simply assertive. By assertively saying that I needed the teachers' help, I was showing that I wanted to know how to partner and consistently follow up on our status. I had lofty expectations for seeing progress. Remember, I wrongly assumed that if there were shortcomings in private school, the school would immediately jump into action and provide my son and me with a plan that would be worked on at school and home, if needed. Once I got over that misconception, I realized that just as there are good teachers, good schools, and good curriculums, there are also opposites and everything in between. I knew I needed a plan to engage routinely. I started with questions.

GETTING INVOLVED - ASKING QUESTIONS

(1.) How is my son/daughter doing in class?

Keep questions open-ended, not indicating or steering in any one particular area so that the answers received might be more holistic. Note: Do not stop with answers that are solely based on socialization. I found that my child's Kindergarten teacher, very kindly, defaulted by responding with, "he is a kind and polite boy." Though I was glad to receive such a response, I needed to know how he was progressing academically as well.

Note: In many schools there are 4 quarters in an academic school year. The number of quarters could vary by state and school system. In general, these quarters are divided into two semesters. The 1st and 2nd quarters fall in the first semester, typically from September through December. The 3rd and 4th quarters are in the 2nd semester, typically from January through June. Report Cards are distributed each quarter, and final grades are released at the end of each semester. Several concepts can be introduced within a month, and understanding the next subject can often require cumulative knowledge of the previous month's concepts. Try to engage with teachers, at minimum, every 2-3 weeks via phone, in person, or by email. If there is a known problem, it may be prudent to engage weekly or bi-monthly. Partnering towards a plan could be just the push needed for a child to receive the extra help needed, feel better about school participation, and be less reluctant to attend school and classes.

Overall, there were early occurrences that taught me that whether the school was private or public, I could not leave my child's progress to chance. When asking probing questions, I was supported by the school system to receive the information I needed and to guide the best help and direction for my child. Next, ask your teacher if they have the time to discuss a possible plan, whether virtual, in person, or via phone. Please try to have this teacher/counselor conversation absent from your child or other students in the classroom. If unable to ask these questions in person, don't forgo asking the right questions. Consider email or voicemail but establish a routine of inquiry and ask the questions. While being in person is always desirable, it is not always the most feasible. Again, the most important thing is showing the teacher you are involved and discussing your child's progress routinely. Doing so, you are more likely to develop a relationship with the teacher that will produce the assistance your child needs.

(2.) What do you suggest we do so my son/daughter can get on the proper track again? Is there a particular plan you would recommend?

The value of this question's composition is two-fold:

1. By acknowledging the teacher's desire for professional assistance with a plan, you also acknowledge their role as a needed support system.

2. Acknowledging the overall partnership effort that you believe exists between the school, the child, and an involved/engaged parent. One thing that should never be understated is that children of parents who are visible and who regularly speak with (not at) their child's school are more likely to receive assistance for their children. Forgive me if "not at" may sound offensive, but every piece of essential advice to me centers around partnering with schools, hoping those efforts will start

on positive grounds and end on higher ground. This method of questioning informs the teacher that you want to be a part of and involved in the solution and have high expectations for your child. With this being said, I must acknowledge that occasional resistance from teachers and schools may exist. Yet even then, there are ways to apply particular care to "soften" the situation and receive the same results. We will address this later in the **Communications Section**.

(3.) End the conversation with a bit of TLC – Thanks, Lock-in, Commit.

a) **Thank You.** Begin to close your exchange with "Thank you." "Thank you" has so much significance when sincerely offered. It allows those who have provided you with valuable information, their time, and their advice to know you value them and their investment in you. I would not begin to close the conversation without including a thank you, knowing that an investment of one's time, no matter how small, is an investment that might be able to help my child's future. Remember to try not to judge the teachers /counselor/principal harshly. People will vary just as there is a difference in professional knowledge and their aptitude and willingness to assist you. I can not stress enough to be respectful. It's essential to have teachers and the school system know that you are a partner AND advocate for your student's well-being. Teachers exchange "personal notes" with other teachers, and you do not want one unruly behavior or interaction to taint the way the school system or its employees treat you. This, unfortunately, can make others less willing to go the extra mile to assist you when needed. Be sincere and show gratitude.

b) **Lock In**. Restate what you believe you have heard: the school and home plan to increase your child's success. For example, "You will provide my daughter/son a weekly worksheet so that she/he can get more practice in a particular "subject" area. When they turn this in, you will grade it with their normal work and provide guidance. In your feedback, you will share if there is additional help you can offer or suggest. I will share our plan with my son/daughter and review the worksheets at home if I can help. Did I miss anything?". This exchange will allow you and the teacher/principal/counselor to review what has been discussed in case of additions or an earlier misunderstanding in the agreed path forward.

c) **Commit and Check-Ins.**

Ensure that you express your commitment to assisting in the path to correction, summarize what you understand as the next steps, and seek agreement on how to follow up for ongoing feedback/exchange.

For example, I promise (or you have my word) that I will work with my son/daughter to make this (the plan) happen. I want to follow up with you to ensure we remain on the proper path and see if we need to adjust. What is the best way or time for us to connect again?

| STORY TIME - |
| INVOLVED: MONITORING AND MANAGING ABSENTEEISM |

My son's school district used an electronic attendance application with certain triggers that were set to notify parents when predefined actions occurred. I remember receiving an evening notification that my son missed a class. In my mind I was saying "Boy, you know better! I know you weren't trying to miss class and believe that I would not know • ??" When I spoke to my son about the system call that I had received that evening, he assured me that there must have been a glitch in the system because he had not missed any classes. The next day, when I contacted the school (notice I was not going to make my decision based on my son's word or the automated system), I learned that my son had attended a class but somehow, he was lollygagging and entered minutes after the late bell. I later learned that my son was actually less than 2 minutes late, but this teacher wanted to "teach him a lesson" about being on time.

Teaching moment for my son: This teacher never stopped or slowed instruction. She never made a comment about him entering the class after the bell, but she was actually "talking" to him in her decision to count him absent instead of late. I needed my son to know that although he felt like the teacher was not being completely honest her opinion would prevail. Knowing that there are colleges that use student attendance as a part of acceptance criteria, my son quickly made the adjustment. There were a few lessons learned. First, the school had a very casual policy in the independence that students had to move between classes, and it even encouraged a policy where students and teachers used first names only within their classrooms. Though my son's other teachers only cared about him earning good grades, this teacher expressed her perceived role to impart a life lesson. I could not help but agree with her.

Though this school gave their students great independence in general, it helped my son to see that there is always a personal element to what a person, though a part of a group, perceives as what is proper. It's important to note that had I not received a call home or there was no checking of the student portal prior to the end of the semester, these absences (though in class) would have been a part of his permanent record. My son, with my urging, asked the teacher privately to consider removal of the absences based on his tardiness but no absences. This occurrence was a large reminder to both he and I to review the parent and student portals more intently.

TEACHER ABSENCES

In 2022, 44% of public schools reported being understaffed.[8] In a similar study of teachers in the school district, 63% of those teachers expressed that they had no plans to return to the school. The United States is facing a crisis in that there are not enough teachers to teach the population of students who need teachers. In most cases, classrooms are severely overcrowded, likely contributing to high levels of teacher burnout. Teachers, too, are beginning to feel the "pinch" of overcrowding and are taking their own time off! Substitute teachers are in limited supply, so depending on the school district's management, that classroom might be without a teacher, added to the numbers of another class, or perhaps even staffed by a substitute who does not possess the academic background or credentials to teach the class as needed.[9] Unsurprisingly, such change can bring about different feelings within students.

School-age children who attend school outside of the home may spend over 70% of their waking hours in school. Since there are now more suggestions that the emotional wellness of children may be equally or more critical to their academic well-being, this knowledge begs the attention of what impact stability has in the lives of children. Whether at home or in school, children are known to seek stability. Since school is where students spend most of their day, whether knowingly or unknowingly, students may find support in teachers who consistently show up for them. To some students, teachers who are consistently absent may subconsciously convey a message that the teacher does not believe in the students' abilities or has given up on their ability to succeed. Children need to know that they are supported and that someone thinks they can succeed despite any obstacles. This is why it is even more important that parents actively cheer their children in academics and social well-being.

---

8   National Center for Education Statistics, (2022).
9   Tan et al., (2024).

Routinely, parents should readily invest time reassuring children of their ability to win against the odds. This is because children may need but not receive more emotional support at school. Due to the sheer number of students in a classroom, parents must contribute to feelings of being seen and not simply being among a large pool of students in a school where acknowledging uniqueness within their individuality may be a non-existent occurrence. While families cannot avoid the impact of teacher absence, one can be prepared to bridge the lack of encouragement and support. Parents can positively support their students by offering emotional encouragement and perhaps supplementing the learning experience with workbooks and online learning tools. Most importantly, as a parent, when you understand that there is high teacher turnover or absence communicated from your student, know there is an opportunity to circumvent learning loss that can ensue due to the frequent absence of teachers. Try to assist in ways you can and seek the support of others if needed.

UNSAFE SCHOOLS

The question of safeness within schools is a growing concern. Bullying and the retaliation that can result is no longer something that can be confined to any one demographic. The growing reality is that people who feel left out, isolated, embarrassed, alienated, envious/jealous, or are seeking more attention can quickly develop feelings of anger. Anger can sometimes lead to bullying in schools. If the intensity of such behaviors is overwhelming against students, this may deter them from going to school. There is help.

Bullying is a severe topic in K12 schools. For this reason, most schools have policies that govern what constitutes bullying, the consequences, and what children and parents should do if they believe they are being bullied. In all cases, the teacher, principal, and district are responsible for protecting the student from such occurrences. The first step is that you, as the parent or your child, make an effort to request change within a hostile environment so that the element of extreme discomfort can be reduced or eliminated.

Secure a copy of the school's policy if you suspect bullying is occurring with your child. Usually, this policy can be found on the school district's website as a first choice, and if it is not found there, search the individual school's website. If unable to locate the policy online, one of my favorite people (and yours too now – the front desk executive administrator) should be your next phone call. Simply ask, "Can you tell me where I might find school policies on classroom and school conduct, such as bullying? Don't be concerned about the complexity of language in the policy because school districts understand that such a policy should be readable by all members of their populations. Again, when reading the policy, seek:

1. The district's broad definition of what bullying is. Ask yourself, "Does this parallel what your child is explaining in any way?"

2. What actions does the policy recommend if one suspects bullying? Who should be consulted or alerted, and how?

3. What type of responses can one expect once the report is made?

What you as a parent must know about bullying is that your intervention can be the help your child has been hoping and praying to receive. Bullying can consume the minds of children when it occurs, and few know that there is a way out and that their pain and discomfort matter. Some bullying can be so intense that children see no way out of the scrutiny that the bully uses to target them. Unfortunately, suicide attempts and death can be the extreme result of such occurrences. For this reason, don't give up on an intervention. You can expect that the teacher will be responsive once you are informed. The school's policy will likely guide the teacher or the point of contact to take immediate and concrete action. There should be an urgency to address poor behavior because liability can be associated with the school's slothfulness to act. Yet, like anything in life, there are informed and uninformed employees and engaged and unengaged employees. The constant is your need for change and your tenacity to find the person, in authority, that can assist in times that require change.

Having a copy of the district's bullying policy and reading what actions are expected of you as a parent will give you access to what should happen in such events. As you convey the behavior to the school, whether through the teacher or principal, remember to ask your point of contact: "As you might imagine (or might know), I am concerned about my son/daughter. Can you follow up with me on our progress soon, or when would you like me to follow up? I cannot stress enough that your conversation should always remain professional and friendly if possible. Remember, in most cases, the teacher you speak to has hundreds of students they see daily and multiple meetings. However, most teachers get into the educational field to help children and will want to help. If you approach them calmly and respectfully, you can expect your approach to stand out and receive a positive response.

Lastly, make a log of your communications. When you spoke, who you spoke with, what was discussed, and what was decided? Such efforts should have a clear intervention path, but documentation will support escalation if needed. If the teacher does not follow up at the time promised, try calling back, but if you are still waiting for a response in a reasonable time, escalate to the principal. If the principal is not assisting you, making the superintendent aware (in writing) is the next level of awareness. Even if difficult, remain professional and express your concern and desire for assistance to keep your child safe. Finding an empathetic advocate who understands the school's need to protect your child will be easier. Similarly, it may also be easier for astute educators to protect your child and the school district from possible litigation. No matter the motivation to assist, your child will receive the intervention needed to negate their fear and return them to regular school attendance and participation.

STORY TIME -
FROM ONE PARENT TO ANOTHER: MY OWN EXPERIENCE
WITH BULLYING IN MY CHILD'S AFTERCARE PROGRAM

I wasn't shocked when my son told me about being pushed regularly and hit in the head by another student in an after-school program. My son was smart, he dressed well and could blend in with any of the cool kids. Somehow, I knew his smartness would not be comfortable for some students.

Soon after my son informed me, I asked the after-school teacher if he would be willing to talk to me privately. To my surprise he wasn't receptive at all. Instead, he began to talk to me about his personal belief that "boys will be boys" and that experiencing something like this was a part of growing up. I didn't believe that at all. While there is some truth to "boys will be boys" I didn't believe, in my son's tween years, that physical touch should be a part of those lessons. Since I felt that this teacher wasn't going to help me, I moved on to speak to the after-school administrator. She assured me that she would talk with the teacher and address the behaviors. Unfortunately, within days my son informed me that their hitting and pushing had not stopped.

As a parent I had to make the tough decision to tell my son that though I did not believe in fighting, he did have the right to protect himself. Shortly thereafter my son pushed the child back and the teacher had to intervene. That afternoon when I arrived, I noticed that my son was not participating in the after-school homework review activities. This troubled me because it was a time where children could ask questions about academic concerns. Instead, he and another young boy were isolated on the other side of the room. When I asked the teacher what happened, he explained to me that he had to step in to calm the two boys and he punished them both. I did not feel as though the other child was going to stop so I thanked the teacher but decided that speaking to the Program director (or principal) would be my next step. After speaking with her, I could sense that she agreed with me, but it did not seem that she wanted to intervene with her long-time male teacher. It was in that moment that I was able to hear what the teacher had expressed to me, what I vehemently disagree with, and it is that "young boys need to be raised much tougher to prepare them for the world that they will meet."

Though both the teacher and Program director knew that my son was being mistreated, each felt differently than I about the experience. This was one of the rare times when I had to begin a new hunt to find after-school care elsewhere. Since I no longer felt like this after-school program would make the decisions that I thought would be beneficial to my child's well-being I decided it was time to move on. Since the after-school program was not in a formal school setting, I opted not to escalate further. Luckily, I was able to find another after-school program that I felt more closely aligned with my values and expectations. I absolutely realize that all parents may not have the ready ability to make such a decision. It certainly was a bit disruptive for me, but I suggest that you not hesitate if you feel like the setting your child is in is not supportive of what you believe to be a safe, or conducive environment for learning or play. It certainly wasn't an easy decision, and I didn't want to feel like I had given up but all the while I knew that moving him was the best choice.

Both the federal and state governments understand that bullying victims can experience reduced academic interest, mental impact, and physical challenges. In most cases, parents find schools very responsive to using this language in communications to advocate for students. Be consistent in your language, i.e., My child has explained what I believe is bullying in Ms. Jones' class. It is impacting/I do not want this to impact my child. What can we do to help [child's name]. Below, I am sharing a few websites loaded with more information to review at your leisure.

- STOPBULLYING.GOV
- THEBULLYPROJECT.COM
- CYBERSMILE.ORG

ACADEMIC EMBARRASSMENT

When children fall behind in class, some do not understand the gravity of not speaking up during class to seek help. Others may be embarrassed to do so. Instead, they fall further and further behind. Of course, this leads to an inability to fully participate in classroom activities. When a teacher calls on this student to answer a question in class, a persistent failure to answer questions asked can lead to a child's complete disengagement. Depending on the child, this embarrassment can cause the student to become overwhelmed. To avoid embarrassment, some students default to the natural response of skipping class or not coming to school at all. Certainly, as parents, we want to prevent this unfruitful response. However, if we're not able to do so, we need to be able to quickly identify a child's disengagement as a possible response to being overwhelmed. In those cases, use the school's resources to determine how you might begin an intervention for your child. In some cases, if you have been monitoring your child's academic progress, the gap might be small and more easily recoverable than the child might have thought possible.

LACK OF FAMILY RESOURCES

A) HOUSING AND TRANSPORTATION

The Current Population Survey (CPS) estimates that single parent households in 2023 were approximately 9.8 million.[10] Those single-parent families are usually dependent upon one paycheck to support the family's needs, and, as a result, there can be resource constraints.

---

10   US Census, (2024).

Some families move often out of necessity to find a lower rental cost for a family dwelling. These relocations can contribute to the loss of education days. In addition, for families with children that do not have transportation to school via the school, money to purchase bus tickets and maintain a car can also get in the way of a child going to school regularly. I cannot stress enough the importance of communicating with the school to convey some of the hurdles that you may face privately. There are often resources less widely advertised to support needs.

B) FOOD AND HEALTH

Moreover, studies support the need for children to be well nourished to concentrate and absorb the information being presented to them in school. Several schools offer school-wide nutritional programs, while others offer children more targeted food plans. Unfortunately, some students come to school on Mondays after a hard weekend of hunger. Some schools also have resources to provide nutrition during the weekend. Again, these programs are not always advertised openly. Please be sure to ask should you need assistance. Try checking the school website and reaching out to the school secretary.

C) CLOTHING

Story time!! I can certainly remember the pressure I felt to dress my son in the most current fashions, including Jordan tennis shoes. Talk about overwhelm!! I felt like I was in a no-win situation. Early on, I'd have to risk not having enough money for the month so my son might wear a pair of Jordans. (Don't judge me). Though I had often reminded my son that his value came from within and not from the outside, I still remembered my peer pressure to wear trendy clothes in K12 to fit in. I recall being recognized in the Senior year classroom superlatives as Best Dressed. I was in shock then, but in hindsight my family certainly was not one that could not have put that money (spent on my clothes) to other uses. Buying my son his first Jordan tennis shoes was definitely a time when I allowed my past to impact my parenting. While being transparent, there was a part of me that wanted my son to experience quality in products early so that he would appreciate the value of quality as opposed to quantity.

For so many years, the tennis shoe was demonized in poor communities. While one may not believe a child with horrible grades who has not applied himself at all should be showered with high-priced clothing, I do believe that all children want to express their uniqueness through their choices of clothing. Some cultures specifically consider the tennis shoe as a part of the preferred outfit and one that is associated with a level of admiration and respect. Since I was from another generation, I could have certainly ignored the impact of a new generation on my child, but that would have been to ignore a part of him that he valued. I did not want that for our relationship.

Clothing can be a very influential factor in how others perceive you. Children know this incredibly early in life and want a part of that influence from their peers. Wardrobing children can be challenging. Whether it is governing what they wear (styles) or having enough choices for them to select from their closets, children want a say. For me, during the early part of my single journey, money was not plentiful; however, I knew that I wanted my son to taste quality clothing. Looking around me, my pocket was not supporting the good life but the "necessities" of life. All that said, much peer pressure is often associated with wearing clothes considered a part of the generation. Assuring children that their worth will far surpass the lifetime of tennis shoes may be a worthwhile approach, but knowing that such pressure could contribute to a child wanting to stay out of school is information that can be valuable in supporting a child past a perceived obstacle.

PRACTICAL STEPS TO REDUCE ABSENTEEISM

In summary, do not choose to keep your child out of school lightly. Here is a thought: As a leader on your job, you are likely very aware when you return from a vacation or multiple days off that there will be communication to catch up, probably new deadlines, and, in general, more work to do than when you departed for time away. K12 students, comparatively, have no less than 4-6 bosses/classroom teachers they would have missed in a day. Any new or enhanced training that might have occurred and any assignment they were given during their absence must be satisfied. Let's say a new concept was introduced in a classroom during an absence, and there is no action taken to reintroduce or review that concept; a student faces an open door that could lead to academic overwhelm.

Children respond to overwhelm differently just as adults. Some rise to the occasion and will do the extra work needed to catch up, and others will be less structured and "hope" that what they did not get during an absence will somehow work itself out. Yet, for some students, the extra work is not done, and success in school becomes a fleeting target. Some parents can assist their children in some way if they have an academic background, but even when they do, their method may not be the one the teacher uses, which can potentially confuse the student further. Unfortunately, students who are absent more and have parents who cannot assist them with their academic time loss are inevitably more likely to fall behind.

RECOMMENDATIONS

RECOMMENDATIONS AND REMINDERS:

VACATIONS

- Consider the loss of learning, the length of time out of classes, and the number of classes that will be missed.
- Timing Is Everything. Try to avoid school days. Consider staycations during the normal school period. Not optimal but this delay will allow your student to continue to thrive.
- Consider alternative dates if possible.

- Winter break vacations (Sunny discounts). Advantage: School is out, and no classes are missed. Few teachers give winter break homework, but don't forget to ask your child. Every grade counts.
- Summer break vacations Advantage: School is out, and no classes will be missed. There is no homework to be missed or considered.

RELOCATIONS

- Moving can require time away from the classroom. Instead chose:
  - Weekend moves over weekday interruptions.
  - If you must move during the weekday, seek to plan a way for your child to arrive at school despite the move schedule.
- Lease expirations (if applicable).
  - Ask the landlord for an amicable month in case moving within a 12-month period is not desirable.
  - Moving during the summer or winter breaks will allow a 12-month lease to expire at a more opportune time.

SUSPENSIONS

- According to some studies, black Students are 3 times more likely to be suspended or expelled than white students.[11] While making the distinction may be uncomfortable for some, as a woman of color and parent, I found this statistic alarming. Assuming that black students are not doing anything wrong 3X more than their peers, this is a clear indication that suspension may impact students unexpectedly.
  - Most schools will make provisions for students who are suspended to receive instruction. It is crucial that you, as a parent, ask, "How will instruction continue for my child?" I do

---

11   Fievre, (2021).

not want them to miss homework or instruction. Is there an online class format, perhaps? What format or process is being used?" Assume the best when asking and advocating for your child. First, it shows your involvement but also asks a very credible question of continuing education.

HEALTH AND WELLNESS CHECKS

- Doctors' visits are a necessity for children in K12. Many times, there are immunization requirements for schools districts. There is, in some states, an option to opt out of the immunizations for religious reasons, but in the majority of cases, parents must make arrangements to comply with such related attendance policies. To add, there are sometimes, no matter how many vitamins we give, children will need routine checkups, sick visits, and other doctor's visits. When doctor appointments are needed, make an effort to avoid or reduce your students' time out of class if your child is *not* ill. Doing so will require you to know your child's school schedule. Of course, if your child is ill all of the planning goes out of the window. Get your child to the doctor as soon as feasibly possible.
- Sickness can require time out of school. As soon as your child knows that he/she will be absent, remind them to reach out to the teacher or a reliable classmate for homework assignments and reading in case your student feels better and is able to complete any of the assignments.

FINANCIAL NEEDS

- Clothing – Instill in students that their real value is within. If there are items that your child wants and you want to deliver, consider thrift stores and 2nd hand shops. There are many items that can be found there that are brand new or gently worn. Wash well and make it your own.

- **Transportation –**
    - If your child is old enough, some public transportation offers discounts for school-age children. In some cases, schools or local states have made arrangements for such discounts to be passed on to parents.
    - Carpools – If there is another parent in the neighborhood that has a working car (if you do not), consider asking if your child can join. Your child will likely enjoy the company. Pay something towards gas to help with the costs of the pickup. I trusted my son with only a few parents. We either gave each other gas money or promised to drive the next time the kids needed rides.
    - School resources – Convey your needs. The school may have resources to assist.

CHAPTER 3

EARLY BIRDS THE POWER OF A STRONG HEAD START IN EDUCATION

INTRODUCTION:

One of the more contemplated decisions a parent must make is when to begin exposing their children to some level of formal education. I struggled with whether I should send my son directly to preschool or *graciously* extend an offer for his amazing grandparents to babysit him while I returned to work after pregnancy. Ultimately, my pockets were saying "grandparents," but for me, I also loved the idea of continuing to socialize with my son. With his grandmother, I knew, without a shadow of a doubt, that she would read to him, love him, protect him, and guide him. She was a Christian through and through, and I loved having her influence surround my son during the day while I went to my 9-5 job. The one thing I recall standing out the most about her is that she had such a calm spirit, and I wanted my son to adopt this attribute (back then, I honestly cannot say I had it).

About months into dropping him off and picking him up after work, I instinctively knew that my young 2-year-old was much more than his grandparents had bargained for. He was all over the house, and his grandparents were getting up in age. They tried to keep up with him, but I could tell he was too much for them. I had to quickly make a change. Prior to making my decision, I weighed the special care my son could potentially continue to receive from his grandparents against the possibility of taking him into an unfamiliar environment with new people, none of which I knew. Ultimately, my love for his grandparents and their care led to my decision to move to a more formal learning setting for my son. I wish I could honestly say that it was because I conducted research and found that taking this action might have a positive influence on his life. Unfortunately, I can't say that, but I can say that transitioning to a formal learning environment yielded positive additions to my son's life that I had not foreseen.

3 CHOICES FOR RECOMMENDATIONS

If we conceptualize K12 as a race and the finish line as graduation, there must be markers on the athletic track for where a student *should be* in their academic progress. In K12, benchmark testing often checks these "markers" throughout the year. There are at least three academic decision areas where parents can potentially have a direct impact on their student's opportunity to progress academically.

Home Life Culture: Early exposure to foundational subjects, specifically English and Math.

ENGLISH AND WORD EXPOSURE

Part of preparing a child to enter K12 at the Pre-K or K levels happens at home. For students who are from families that are less fortunate or severely economically challenged, studies suggest that children may not receive the same frequency and quality of communication from their parents in the home when compared to parents who are accustomed to more advantage.[12] There could be many contributors to the possible limitations in exposure to usable words within the home. Lower-income families may have a higher level of stress associated with their lifestyles, partially due to the need to work more hours outside of the home environment. Yet this deficiency, seen in lower-income families, is not confined to income because higher-paid parents may also be out of the home more due to work hours. Stress, language, and energy associated with such environments are not always conducive soil that young children can become enriched when planted within these environments. The result is that children from *some* homes could be more prone to enter schools with comparatively limited exposure to words and have a more sizable learning curve in kindergarten influenced by that lack.

Not hearing words routinely can have other impacts. Larry Bell, who was nominated for the National Agnes Meyer Outstanding Teacher Award, wrote in his book "12 Powerful Words" that he remembers when he discovered some standardized assessments contained words in their question that students and even a few teachers did not know.[13] Teachers cannot help students while taking a standardized test, even if it comes to students asking them the meaning of a particular word or question on the test. Words and definitions like "infer – reading between the lines" or "formulate – to create something" are included in the 12 words to recognize, referenced in Bell's book. Finally, word exposure is something parents should keep at the top of their minds

12   Ellwood-Lowe et al., (2020).
13   Bell, (2005).

as it is a building block to future learning. It is a way to help children soar that is not confined by parental income or zip code.

There are several practical practices parents can incorporate to increase word exposure early. Since English is one of the two core subjects, parents will want to incorporate opportunities to feed their children's early academic progress. To take advantage of this opportunity to teach early, parents are encouraged to be more intentional about talking more around *and to* their children. Children are always listening and observing even when we may not want them to. What might be "slang" to an adult and consistently in a joke or in common exchanges can potentially become the main words for a child who is like a sponge, absorbing all that is heard.

Similarly, as parents, it's so easy to stay in the place of connecting to younger children using small talk or babble as children are experimenting and quickly building their communication skills. If a child is only hearing words that are not transferable to other settings for months at a time while another child is read to and spoken to much earlier, such engagement can contribute to a wider disconnect in social and academic adaptability later. There is no shortage of social media posts where children have been exposed to music with profane language and parents are entertained because they can recite a song at a very young age. Retention and learning are traits that parents desire in their children. However, trying to *unlearn* and remove words that may not be appropriate in other settings may be too complex for young minds, especially if they are rewarded for profanity or lower-quality language in the home. This does not condemn baby-talk, trending music, and colloquialisms and their value. Instead, this is an opportunity to highlight the importance of exposure to words found in the dictionary to broaden children's word arsenal and memorization in ways that will be helpful to them very early and throughout their K12 years.

The mere fact that so many children learn music videos and songs might suggest that exposing children to other activities that they enjoy, which have elements of teaching counting and word recognition, is a possible source for the growth of their academic foundations. For instance, using age-specific internet applications for reading that are delivered in ways that keep children's attention is one way to seek their focus to participate in an activity they find enjoyable while learning. Applications such as IXL and Lexia are just a few examples that use lively graphics and varied delivery methods to keep student engagement high. Reading books and allowing students to begin to associate spoken words with the words that are in print is also a very practical way to participate in increasing word exposure. Including closing conversations about the lessons and characters of the book also provides more opportunities for word exposure and deeper relationship development between parent and child.

The words that parents speak to children to support their learning efforts are not completely academically based but of equal importance. Parents must instill in their children a belief that there are no limitations on what they can learn and do if they invest time and effort. A parent's faith in their child's ability to do anything propels children to believe that they can excel. While teaching your students foundational words, remember to feed their spirits with words of encouragement. Parents are among the most influential factors in a student's belief system.[14] Seek to reward your children often by speaking light into them and letting them know that you are their biggest cheerleader, their advocate.

COUNTING AND NUMBER RECOGNITION AT HOME

Equally important is exposing young children to numbers and simple mathematical concepts. When children are introduced to mathematical concepts at an early age, their brains are believed to become conditioned to thinking analytically.[15] Such efforts as introducing the number of feet, toes, and ears allow children to begin grasping the

---

14   New America Media, (2014).
15   Clements and Sarama, (2009).

association of one to many. Flashcards for basic mathematical concepts such as addition, subtraction, and multiplication help with recall. This is also an inexpensive way to spend quality time with students while helping them build their math muscle. Repetition learning, like using flashcards, can be controversial for some who believe that repetition only promotes memorization. However, I believe that memorizing basic math concepts allows the brain to be freed so that analytics and more advanced applications are much easier later. One of the places where this is more pronounced is in middle school. Many students reach middle school *without* knowing their multiplication.[16] This has a profound impact on their ability to perform well in common curriculum classes such as algebra. Further, without a suitable mathematical background, students may continue to struggle to keep up with the increasing complexity of math encountered in later high school grades, hindering their overall academic progress and threatening their ability to perform well in college.[17] Young students will want to have early and repeated familiarization with basic math concepts such as addition, subtraction, multiplication, and division so that participating in advanced mathematics when time allows, is a possibility. Mathematical exercises such as using flashcards, counting coins, and their own body parts (nose, eyes, ears) are very accessible ways to invoke learning in this area. Similarly to word exposure, online applications have also been created for younger age groups.

PREK AND K

During the year this book was written, seventeen states (including the District of Columbia) require students to begin their academic journeys by attending either full-time or part-time kindergarten.[18] For all the states that do not require Kindergarten, this generally means that 9-10 months of learning and socialization are absent from a student's development. Just a somewhat rhetorical question

---

16   Chamorro, (2021).
17   Adelman, (2006).
18   Education Commission of States, (2023).

or food for thought: "Could 9-10 months of structured curriculum yield noticeable gains when compared to the student that did NOT attend?" It's very possible. In fact, there are some suggestions that falling behind in kindergarten, without effective intervention, follow students throughout their K12 experience, contributing to low grades and class failures. In contrast, quality Pre-K programs are associated with producing positive, long-term academic impact throughout the term of the K12 experience.[19] For instance, students who participate in pre-k programs are more likely to graduate high school and move on to college.[20] No doubt, Kindergarten entry is a sensitive time in the child's developmental process.

In the Pre-K setting, children not only begin to learn educational concepts earlier but have more of an opportunity for immersion into other areas that begin to develop them holistically. Students are not only learning new words and concepts from their teachers but also participating in new social interactions with their peers. Children learn the concepts of sharing, resolving conflict, and exchanging words to express themselves in ways that allow them to experience different responses and reactions from varied peer groups. Similarly, students, when placed in a diverse Pre-K or K setting, have more opportunity to begin early socialization in settings that are more representative of the world adults daily navigate, and they will later enter. Overall, early education programs such as Pre-K and K help children begin to develop much-needed skills and exposure in the areas of language and literacy, mathematics, problem-solving, culture, and social interaction. Of course, there are competing alternatives to Pre-K. I know because I chose one of them. I opted to have my son stay with his grandmother during his Pre-K years because I wanted to know that he would be raised in a nurturing environment. I also wanted his immune system to grow stronger, which I associated with being in a smaller home environment. I cannot say that I made the wrong choice because he accomplished those things, but when he arrived

---

19   Duncan et al., (2007); Duncan and Magnuson, (2011).
20   USDOE, (2015).

in kindergarten, I believe he needed to work twice as hard to catch up academically.

We were able to intervene because he had a responsive teacher who worked with us and was so vigilant to observe and exchange so that my son remained on target. We were able to have the best of both worlds: family care and structured education outside of the home. My son not only caught up but exceeded expectations because it was in those very years that I discovered that I would ensure certain concepts were either introduced to him or consistently exposed to him at home. I learned that the education system, being overcrowded, overlooked my students' needs at times. He was much too young to know how to articulate any possible need. Needless to say, he excelled! He did so with great strides, but looking back, I firmly believe this extra work was necessary because he missed that year of Pre-K preparation. I often think, what if I were not a parent who knew the importance of routinely asking about my son's progress and the school allowed him to blend in with everyone else because of a large class size, the outcome could have been completely different. In this case, I needed to ask questions about my son's progress and ask for specific guidance on what we, the school system and I, could do to help him get back on track.

Highly recommended: Ask questions. Ensure your student's teacher knows your voice throughout the year and not just at report card time. Report cards should not be a surprise whether a parent opts to use technology-based grade books or whether manual meetings and conversations are solely used.

CHAPTER 4

ADMINISTRATIVE ANCHORS THE BACKBONE OF SCHOOL OPERATIONS

At first thought, I resisted the notion of referring to the employee roles of the school system as its academic players. Still, as I looked closer, I grew less concerned about associating the mastery of navigating the school system as a type of game. I became less concerned because I honestly believe the more you know about the school system, the better you are able to help your child excel, avoid its pitfalls, and navigate to grasp the many treasures of the K12 experience. Just as the action of knowing what the rules of a game are and the proven movements to win (the associated processes and policies), it is equally as important to understand and recognize the major players (those employed by and working closely with the school system) within the ever-changing landscape (*game)* of participating in K12. I have to add that using the word "game" is also appropriate because in any well-known game, those who know the board and the power of the movement within the board win the prize far more frequently than those who enter the game haphazardly and leave themselves and in this case their children, to fate. Both public and private K12 systems have much to offer, some more than others. I quickly found that learning the roles within the school would mean the difference between a poor, average, or above-average experience. Much like you, I wanted to learn what tools and knowledge I needed to be aware of and when to utilize or seek them out to help my student arrive at their best.

The role of key employees in the K12 system: In this chapter we identify the "players" within the K12 setting as well as their importance in fostering stability and growth within a child's academic and social lives.

TEACHERS

Teachers are at the "heart" of the K12 system. They are responsible for planning and delivering instructional lessons to students, closely monitoring the overall progress of the classroom, identifying any shortcomings within a student's academic progress, and offering solutions for students who are in need. By far, teachers are the resource with which children interact the most and are most trusted by the school district to present grade-level content in a way that will result in student learning. Since teachers are by far one of the most influential resources in students' academic progress, the relationship between student and teacher is one of high value and potential return. As in all positive relationships, nurturing such relationships requires a clear understanding of both the good and bad characteristics that might impact the quality of the relationship.

There is so much scrutiny associated with what teachers do, especially during and after the pandemic. What is undeniable is that student test scores in most districts plummeted after the pandemic.[21] Students fell behind and school districts scrambled to find a solution to help children recover quality instructional time lost. In the crossfires

---

21   NAEP Long-term Trend Assessment, (2022).

came teacher resignations. Many teachers left the field and for those dedicated teachers that remained, many of them faced larger classrooms with far more students to teach and monitor. In 2024, in the state of Virginia, for instance, 3,600 full-time teacher vacancies were reported.[22] Nevertheless, there has been no shortage of finger-pointing at teachers, many of which are operating in less-than-optimal conditions but feel called to lead children into learning. Certainly, there are highly effective teachers who may not love the profession or perhaps not even the students but still produce outstanding results in the classroom. Just as in any profession, it is not always easy to see with your natural eye what teachers are effective and which are less effective. There are a few attributes that may help to identify teachers who are more likely to be effective in the classroom.

There is no known set of criteria that guarantees a teacher to be able to successfully connect and educate each student. Intentional parental engagement practices and assessment use are two characteristics that are valuable teacher qualities. At the beginning of each year, some students may enter the classroom below where their aptitude should be for the classroom. This condition is an unfortunate reality but a recoverable one in many cases. An important quality for an effective teacher to have has been to understand the value of assessment and the resulting responses that can help students progress and remain on track. Schools often require assessments at various intervals; teachers who are attuned to their classrooms will not only perceive problems early but personally assess and act on those findings (as needed) promptly. Teachers who follow up assessments with ongoing parental engagement, well-thought-out suggestions of potential academic or socioemotional planning, and offer encouraging hope to both parents and students are highly desirable partners to parents.

It is so important to add a caveat and reminder here. Due to the loss of so many teachers, some classrooms can be overcrowded. Overcrowded classrooms require that the remaining teachers manage more

---

22   Richmond.com, (2024).

students. As parents, we can be empathetic to changing conditions and also receive what we need to help monitor our child's progress. By initiating contact with teachers to engage at a mutually agreed upon time to discuss the progress of our individual students, we can help support their academic success. Keep in mind, most teachers of grades 6-12 come in contact with over 70 students in a normal school day. The engaged parent, not the one who is overbearing or inconsiderate, is more prone to receive special attention. Not easy to hear but teachers may respond better to considerate and concerned parents. Reaching out to obtain information, a teacher knows this parent wants to be involved. As such, the teacher can begin to feel confident that they can trust the parent to share good or bad academic or social feedback.

Now, some critics may say "Well, if you did not think you could do the job, why be a teacher and why must parents initiate or be especially nice to teachers?" Agreeing, disagreeing, or initiating with such sentiments, a parent may be easily distracted and miss the "main target," that YOUR child might benefit academically and socially simply by your efforts to partner. Thinking of teachers as partners to help your students and not adversaries is crucial to the mindset that should guide parent interaction with the teacher. Just as in any relationship, respect is paramount to both parties being heard and valued. Further, one of the most valuable lessons we can teach our children is to respect others and conduct ourselves in a way that invokes respect from others. Parents, we have an opportunity to teach our children how to respect time management and the roles of others just by exhibiting respect and professional courtesy when communicating with their teachers.

Now, this may seem obvious or condescending, and that is far from the intention; however, matters with parents advocating for their children can evoke strong emotions. Let's just acknowledge this. Unfortunately, those strong emotions can result in less than admirable occurrences, some even as extreme as evoking violent behaviors from parents and teachers. The strongest emotions are often evoked when parents feel helpless to protect their children or provide them with the necessary resources to progress. This is just another opportunity for parents to demonstrate the power of being consistently kind and the results that often follow. Being mean or disrespectful to a teacher rarely yields the desired result. Remember, students are always learning, and even if the teacher is not conducting him or herself as you expect, the better choice is to remain calm and respectful. There is always an opportunity where a teacher can choose to go the extra mile for a child which may require personal time from the teacher. Most do extra work because of their love for the profession and do so willingly, but it is not required. Unbeknownst to some, teachers often exchange non-confidential information about students. If a parent has mistreated a teacher and that teacher casually mentions such an interaction(s), that parent might be met in next year's classroom by a teacher who is defensive and simply avoids contact with you. Overall, humane and professional interaction often wins in the long term. After all, the decisions we make now to help our children may impact their futures.

Knowing a bit about your child's teacher qualifications, especially when your children are in K- 5, may prove informative to parents for several reasons. During PreK-4th grade, students are generally taught academic subjects by 1-2 teachers for the full school day. Remember this can vary by state and school district. The instructional setting is significant because these years are an optimal time for students to grasp fundamental concepts in many areas, include English and Mathematics. While several subjects are taught within a day in Prek-4, the teacher generally has much autonomy in deciding the amount of time spent on any subject. There could be positives and negatives that show up because of such classroom time decisions. Having a teacher who has a high aptitude in Mathematics or English, a student is likely to spend their day with a teacher who is confident in those subject areas. Naturally, they will gravitate towards spending time in those subjects, and this time may certainly benefit your student as they build their academic background. Additionally, there is a strong likelihood that the teacher will teach with a higher level of accuracy.

The years of a teacher's experience are also considered a factor of teacher quality. Teachers who have three or more years of experience in the classroom are thought to have obtained practical and functional skills to manage their classrooms and promote learning.[23] In contrast, teachers in years 1 or 2 of their careers are more prone to be immersed in applying different theories to determine which might be better suited for them. This in no way would suggest that these teachers are not proficient in their fields in years 1 and 2, but it does consider that there might be a trial-and-error learning curve associated with newly employed teachers. Other characteristics that are desirable are valid teacher certification and academic degree attainment (associate, bachelor's, master's, doctorate). Some states within the United States require that teachers obtain teacher certification and acquire continuing education credits at intervals. The "provisional teacher" is a term used to explain the status of a teacher who is working towards certification with a deadline to achieve such status. Again, these characteristics identified to assist in distinguishing quality teachers are not all-inclusive but provide a compass for parents who are seeking teachers who are more likely to be equipped and engaged. Regrettably, students in poorer school districts are often taught by teachers who do not meet some of these standards of high quality.[24] Lastly, and thought to be significant, is the teacher's willingness to develop professional relationships with their students where they see children as individuals and have a conversation with them. Quite directly, as parents, it may be prudent to learn your student's status in some of these areas. If your child is struggling academically, a good teacher can make all of the difference.

To learn the status of teacher certification, visit the website for the department of education for your state (for instance Baltimore Department of Education teacher certification). Some websites, if provided the first and last names and district, will show teacher certification status. But what happens if you know your teacher is

---

23   Stronge, (2007).
24   Darling-Hammond and Sykes, (2003); Stronge, (2007).

not certified? This does not mean that your child's teacher is not qualified. They may have missed a deadline to complete continuing education, for instance. If your child is struggling to go into a teacher's class and the teacher does not seem engaged or properly prepared after meeting with them or talking to them, asking that your child be transferred to another teacher before or shortly after starting the school semester may be an option. Remember, though teachers are "the heart" of the school, they do not have the authority to perform all the tasks you may desire during your student's academic experience. There are many other impactful employees within the school system.

POINTS TO REMEMBER:

- When a poor-quality teacher is assigned in a grade year, the impact extends several years beyond that one class.[25] Try to review your child's schedule prior to the school opening. Investigate the teacher assigned and if there are no good signs found, consider seeking a transfer to another class. During your investigation, consider asking other older parents and students about their experiences with the teacher. There is a chance that other parents will be quite candid.
- Teachers are the resources who will likely spend the most time with your students. Teacher opinions, because classrooms are so much more than the subjects that are taught there, and likeability, in addition to their subject matter knowledge, may have a high impact on a child's overall well-being. In fact, some researchers have associated a student's willingness to come to school and participate is in direct association to liking their teacher.[26]
- Though the impact of teachers is vast, their power to make some changes is limited, and their time is equally limited. Make certain that you "hear" teachers when she/he expresses their inability to help in a particular area but also simply ask who can help.

---

25   Sanders and Rivers, (1966).
26   White, (2007).

PRINCIPALS

Principals are the accountability leaders of the schools to which they are assigned. One of their top priorities is to provide the overall vision for their building, hire qualified staff, and establish effective operations. Principals are involved, either directly or indirectly, in instructional delivery, in establishing and implementing disciplinary policies, and in managing the school's budget. Principals also act as the core stakeholder that represents the school in the community, with parents and in the school district at large. The superintendent depends on the principal to uphold the academic requirements of the school and the associated school and student policy.

SCHOOL COUNSELORS

School Counselors serve the school in a multi-dimensional capacity, assisting students in (a) academic course selection and schedule planning, (b) college and career readiness, and (c) social and personal development. These professionals can have varied academic backgrounds. Some counselors study psychology, which equips them to support social and personal development in students, while others may opt for childhood development degrees that provide a basis for assisting students towards the direction of their desires and gifting in career readiness. Most elementary schools are required to have two certified counselors in the building throughout the school year based on student numbers. School Counselors are responsible for the planning, support, and counseling needs of several hundred students within the building. This role is mentioned here because it provides one of the more important roadmaps for students, including career development, social and emotional support, and successfully meeting graduation requirements. As with all references, the number of employees can vary by region, district, and funding availability. The number of typically assigned counselors referenced above is based on a subset of school districts in the eastern region of the country.

Of their many responsibilities, counselors organize and deliver student class schedules for the school year. This is a critical task because all students must demonstrate, via school records, that they have met the requirements for graduation. If a student does not attend the proper number and types of classes, which are assigned via class schedules, students do not graduate. This is a critical point to highlight in the academic monitoring process. Counselors also have access to a wealth of information on career choice, and that information, coupled with the academic histories of students, can begin to help students draw their personal visions for career and or college choices. In some cases, strategic course selection during high school can better prepare students to be successful in their college majors by providing early exposure to a higher level of rigor. This is especially thought to be true in mathematics.[27] Unfortunately, some students struggle when moving to college primarily because their college-entry literacy and mathematics skills could be stronger. Knowing this, parents can opt to review schedules so that course levels supporting their long-term goals can be added to their child's middle and high school schedules. If this is your goal, do not assume that it will be done. Make certain that your student has this conversation with the counselor and these classes are included in their planning. Also particularly important to note, high school counselors often know the most about scholarship opportunities. Scholarships are hardly ever all-inclusive, so it is important to get on the counselor's radar early. Ninth grade is not too early to start strategizing with the high school counselor. In fact, some parents start strategizing (identifying the requirements for eligibility for routinely available scholarships) in middle school. Remember, there may be other students hoping for money, but your extra effort to be visible to the counselor may be included on the "top of mind" list when a scholarship is available.

Given the importance of counselors to student planning, student meetings with counselors can easily be a required yearly task. Some schools require such sessions, but others leave the responsibility

---

27   Rose and Betts, (2001); Altonji, (1995).

to initiate such conversations to the student and parent. One of the blockers to establishing mandatory meetings may be the ratio of counselors to students that can exist in larger schools. Students often outnumber counselors by hundreds, so planning yearly meetings with each grade-level student could be a time management challenge. By far, the frequency by which counselors initiate meetings with students and families is dependent upon the counselor's personal style and the direction of the principal or district. In summary, counselors perform a crucial task for students, often behind the scenes, far from the spotlight, and their work produces the desirable outcome of on-time graduation. Yet, there are occasions where a counselor may not prepare a schedule properly, or preparation of proper schedules may not be the sole responsibility of the counselor in the school but is shared with the student. Unfortunately, for those smaller populations of students, on-time graduation can be jeopardized, taken away, or students can be required to take more classes than necessary to graduate.

One of the most heartbreaking things to experience in the high school system is to hear news of the high-school seniors who reach weeks before graduation to discover that they have fewer credits than are required for graduation. Unfortunately, such occurrences are not uncommon. Working in the IT department and viewing the number of families that faced these situations each year was hard to witness, but these numbers can be reduced. There are many ways a student can fall short of graduation eligibility. Please see a few of the more common reasons below.

1. The student is promoted from one grade to another but fails a required class in the grade year before promotion. The failed class is not added to the new year's course load but is missed or replaced by a course that does not meet the current and prior year's requirements.

2. The classes assigned to a student in a given year do not meet the minimum requirements for an individual school year or

overall graduation. For instance, ninth grade may require an earth science class that is three credits, but instead, the student is assigned physical science with three credits.

While the number of students that fall into these categories is small in comparison to those who are assigned schedules that satisfy requirements, no parent or student wants to discover at the end of the 12th grade that they did not meet the needed requirements. Families can take a few steps to make certain the possibility of being included in this number is reduced.

RECOMMENDATIONS:

- In ninth grade, school systems generally arrange for students to meet with the counselor either individually or in a group setting. If parents are invited to join in these meetings, this is time well spent. If this meeting is not scheduled for your students, arrange a meeting with the school counselor. This meeting is so important because it establishes the roadmap for the student's entire high school time period. During this meeting, each parent and student should obtain information and two artifacts:
- The recommended classes for the upcoming school year
- The minimum requirements list for graduation. If the Minimum Requirements for Graduation are not offered in a group setting, ask for them during open questions or email the counselor shortly thereafter asking where these requirements can be found. In most cases, these requirements are found on the individual school's or district's websites. In some cases, the website for the State Board of Education may also be easily searched. At any rate, obtain this copy because this will be the roadmap for the family partnership (student and parent) to follow to confirm that requirements are met each year.
- Each year before the beginning of school, students will receive their course/class schedule. The Minimum Requirements document will detail which classes and credit counts are required for each

year. The minimum requirements document and the yearly course/ class schedule should be reviewed at the beginning of each year. For instance, if the minimum requirement document requires a student to acquire three credits of earth science in the 10th grade, but the student's course schedule contains physical science with three credits, this may be a reason for concern. Do not ignore any concerns or questions. Counselors are more than willing to assist.

▪ Schedule an in-person meeting with the counselor when possible or schedule a phone conversation as a second choice if time does not allow an in-person visit. Follow up on your meeting with the counselor, preferably in writing, so that there is no misunderstanding of the direction conveyed and the path to be taken. Student counselor contacts can be found in one or more of the following ways:

  ▪ Contact the school via phone or email and request the name of the grade-level counselor.
  ▪ Visit the school website.
  ▪ Ask your student to visit the office to make an appointment with the counselor. Note: An opportune time to visit the school office to request an appointment may be during the lunch period.

Counselors also provide a safe haven for students and school staff to discuss social and emotional challenges that they may be facing. In many cases, counselors can identify resources for students to help them or provide a level of direction and wisdom in their personal goals. There will likely be a restraint on the depth of feedback that a counselor can provide without parental presence; however, counselors are generally professionally trained staff members and are depended upon by school systems for guidance. Additionally, counselors provide coping mechanisms in the event of high-stress and traumatizing situations, helping students to successfully navigate challenges.

Points to Remember about Counselors:

- Assistance in selecting the proper course that will allow your child to meet the requirements for graduation.
- Usually, they have input in the selection of students for advanced courses and gifted and talented courses.
- Usually, they have input on the selection of students for dual enrollment. Reminder: Dual Enrollment -students attend college courses while still in high school. It usually occurs in year 11 or 12. These classes can be attractive to parents and students because the high school pays for the college courses; these credits can reduce the cost and length of your student's college degree.
- If your child struggled academically in a particular subject during the previous year, seek consideration to discuss the teachers available for the coming year. Discuss topics like: (a.) Confirmation of certification (b.) Pass/fail rates (c) Past success in similar situations.

TUTORS AND SPECIAL EDUCATION TEACHERS

Other school professionals support teachers in assisting students in creating higher academic standing. Tutors are the school resources assigned to students either in the same classroom or outside of the school to enhance their academic standing. One misconception may be that tutors are only sought by students who fall behind, but tutors are also used to maintain or gain additional ground in the academic realm. In larger public schools, the number of tutors can be limited. Parents monitoring their student's progress and students trained to understand that tutors are a viable source for an alternative teaching experience can make an effort to request these resources early. Often students need an alternative person to present learning materials in a new way for them to grasp a concept that was not understood when introduced by the primary teacher. Parents can help to remove any stigma associated with tutors. Tutors are usually in smaller settings, have dedicated time with a student or a group of students, and are trained in alternative learning methods. The goal is to ensure that students reach the intended learning objective even though their paths to do so may differ.

CENTRAL OFFICE ADMINISTRATOR

Central Office administrators support the overall management of the district and usually report directly to the Superintendent. There can be several roles grouped into this category and the titles of the administrators may vary by district. Each Central Office department lead is expected to understand school district policies and procedures and confirm that such policies are being adhered to within schools. Administrators also ensure goals approved by the superintendent are met by delegating tasks and setting performance expectations. There are far too many administrative titles to name here, but there are a few that require note: Chief Academic Officer, Diversity, Equity, and Inclusion Director, Director of Assessment, Director of Elementary Education, and Director of Secondary Education. One of the more important characteristics to understand about this group of professionals is their influence locally, specific to their school district, and their ability to enforce district-wide policy. Though this group is not normally the first person with which a parent should speak about a concern that a policy is or is not being followed, these roles may have an interest in discussing an event that might have compromised policies that have been established. Overall, this group has a wealth of knowledge and are professionals with several years of experience. The professional title names may vary but there is generally someone within a school district that performs these duties. Finding the title name for your school's district will not be difficult.

DIRECTOR OF TRANSPORTATION

This role is responsible for transportation to and from school as well as transportation within the school day. There is so much that can happen on a school bus. I personally remember being bullied on the school bus because my ponytail happened to be longer than some of the other girls my age. During that time, I do not think bullying came with the policies and repercussions that are now associated. Unfortunately, the ride on some school buses can be far more concerning than a ponytail pull in the 21st century. The bus drivers do not make school policies but are required to uphold the policies while students are on the bus. Depending on the school's structure, contacting the Department of Transportation for the school if poor behavior is occurring might be the best resource. Do not be discouraged if the person answering the phone redirects you to another department. Schools want to know if there is a problem that might also impact other students. Even if the person on the other end of the phone sounds busy and exhausted, be the concerned energy needed to fuel movement and resolutions. As in all situations, I recommend being kind - - even if its difficult. While your child is most important to you and important to the school there could be several other requests being surfaced. If there is a grave concern, always follow up your phone call with a written note via email.

DIRECTOR OF SCHOOL NUTRITION

These professionals manage food preparation for students and staff and usually maintain the budget used for the many types of food purchased. Children who come to school without being hungry during instruction are thought to keep focus longer, absorb more, and perform at higher levels. Unfortunately, food can be restrictive for parents who are suffering due to unemployment or underemployment. If your child has any type of food allergy, there should be an entry in the school nutritional system to make the cafeteria aware. The school can usually confirm this with a simple phone call to the primary office and similar application processes. Lastly, if directors know that there is a need within a family, they may be the ones to seek additional resources to discreetly provide for the family when available.

SUPPORT STAFF:

Support staff members, such as executive assistants, librarians, office assistants, security, nutritional services or cafeteria specialists, transportation office services, and janitors, play crucial roles in the school's daily operations. These roles extend the reach of teachers and often assist students with their daily activities. Support staff also provide administrative and logistical support to ensure that the school runs efficiently. I cannot say this in a bold enough letter: Making friends or acquaintances with your child's school's executive assistant and front desk secretary will have a large return on investment. Let us be clear: being cordial, in my opinion, usually has a return that is favorable; however, there is a human side of us that may rear its ugly head when we are emotional without identifying ways to harness that energy in a positive way. Do not overlook this. The stakes are much higher because we, as parents, can choose to make a potentially positive deposit into our children's learning and well-being by sowing positive things into the lives of those entrusted with their daily lives. This is how I thought of it. Both executive assistants and front desk secretary roles have direct access to one of the busiest resources in the school, the principal. Sometimes, your student's teacher does not have the authority to change or challenge a particular situation, requirement, rule, or ruling. The principal, however, is more likely to have that authority. In many cases, these resources are very aware that a smaller part of their larger values lie within their role of protecting the principal's time and partnering with principals to get things done. Showing these partners respect or sowing respect into them, I received the same respect and benefited from their direction on many occasions.

When my son was in middle school, I received a call from his school during my work hours of 8-4:30 pm. Someone I knew from the office, from intentionally introducing myself and routinely speaking and having genuine exchanges during any visits, was the one who notified me in a phone call by explaining my son was okay but had been in an accident at school. I stopped breathing at that moment. That day, I was able to go directly to the school. There, I found my son with a very obviously swollen face. His teacher told me that he and another young man would be suspended because they were running through the cafeteria and hurting themselves and others after repeated warnings that day. I could speak to my son privately when the teacher left the room. I leaned into him and asked my son if this account was accurate. He told me "No" and that he was not even running at all, but he was hit in the face by the boy as he was entering the cafeteria. The teacher did not believe him and took the stand that it would be fair to suspend both students for a day to make sure other students understood that there were consequences for such behaviors. Though my son had not had any blatant behavior issues in not listening to school authority prior, of which I was aware, I felt like I needed to find the truth for myself and him. I knew there must be a policy that addresses suspension, so I found that policy related to suspensions on my phone from the school website, and I read the policy. I may not have been at the incident when it occurred and might question my son's involvement, but I knew I did not want him to miss the school day. What I interpreted when I read the policy made me believe that suspension only occurred under certain circumstances, and what I was hearing (true or not) did not seem to be one of those circumstances. I wanted a second opinion. Now, this is where it was a bit uncomfortable for me. I believed in the authority of the school system, but I did not want my son to be punished for something he might not have done. I requested a meeting with the principal. From there, I expressed that I believed my son and asked that an extra step be taken. I requested that the school cameras be reviewed. After some moments, the principal hesitantly agreed to consider the video. In the end, the cameras showed just what my son said. He was the victim of a strong hit to the head by someone who was twice his size, and he was, in fact, doing nothing other than walking.

In summary, this section was intended to present a high-level description of some official school roles, but in all situations, here are a few things to know as you navigate the school's system, which includes knowing its players.

Does the person you are speaking to have the authority to make a change, exception, or decision for what you are asking? If not, who else has that authority, and how can you remain professionally poised and request their guidance?

▪ Unless you are in a crisis situation or time crunch, be unwavering in your confidence to simply ask for the guidance that you need from any of the educational resources available to you. Do not feel confined to your child's teachers should you feel that you have an issue not related to instruction. Even if you select someone who cannot directly assist you, you will likely receive new information that you can readily add to your toolkit. Some staff members will genuinely want to help; not everyone in the "helpful" category will be publicly listed on an organizational chart.

  ▪ I would like to say I went to my son's school very often, but I did go there often enough to meet the librarian, cafeteria workers, and, of course, many of the teachers and principal. This may not always be possible, but finding a way to add 2-3 half days minimum per year if you have paid time off to visit your child's school during parent-teacher conference days, showing your face, and making introductions exemplifies an involved and concerned parent. If you are unable to spare the time off to do so, this is only one way to openly demonstrate your involvement in your child's school experience. Most importantly, do not beat yourself up. Be kind to yourself and stay motivated to find ways to advocate for your students. If you are married or have a trusted family member who is able to take time to be at the school during these periods, ask them to partner with you. In order to have an alternate family member visit during parent-teacher conference days, you will need to call the school office to learn what would be the process to add someone in their files that would have access to your child's academic progress and be able to discuss matters of academic and social wellness with their teachers.

- Teachers are most often the school resource that parents have more ready access to and more visibility. If you are reporting a perceived problem, remember the classroom teacher may not be the individual with the authority to deliver the results you desire. If the teacher is not available to you after attempts to reach them, move to the following resource that might be able to assist you. If you have not been able to connect with a resource that is authorized to address your need, ask, "Who might be the individual that can assist me in helping my child with this situation?"

- Start all your pursuits for answers or assistance with the assumption and belief that many teachers enter the field of education because they have a love or compassion for positively impacting the lives of children. They, in general, want to make a difference in the lives of their students. Sure, some may not have entered the field for those reasons, but your mindset should start with believing these types of school partners are in the minority. Remember, school staff members are working within a system that is serving more needs than were present prior to the Pandemic. Classroom behaviors are different, and some children are carrying the weight of home lifestyles that young minds should never be burdened with. Such trauma often presents itself as a disruption to the classroom beyond what one classroom teacher can provide. And what does that mean to you? Teachers and other resources may already be taking on more responsibilities than they were prior and coping in less-than-desirable conditions. However, your focus is to tap into their passion and knowledge and seek it to guide and elevate your child's academic and social journey while in K12.

CHAPTER 5

FROM POLICY TO PRACTICE NAVIGATING FEDERAL AND LOCAL POLICY DYNAMICS

The policy is "a set of ideas or a plan of what to do in particular situations that have been agreed to officially by a group of people, a business organization, a government or political party."[28] Policies are established to increase the odds that any selected process, no matter the location, will produce the same or comparable results. Education has long been governed by both policies originating from the federal and local governments. For education, there are two generic categories to be discussed here: Federal Legislation and Local Policies. Federal policies are rules that apply to several states and are often crafted by higher-order courts. In comparison, local policies are specific to a state, school division, or school. There are a few common federal policies that exist to have far-reaching influence in several states as well.

FEDERAL LEGISLATION AND POLICY

No Child Left Behind (NCLB). Federal legislation can cover many areas. In this section, we will be highlighting only a few. The No Child Left Behind Act was the federal government's effort to implement guidelines throughout the United States public school system that would require student testing to occur in schools and those results to be shared with the federal government. The penalties were high for schools that did not reach acceptable ratings in student test scores. For instance, schools that failed to make a specified pass rate could be required to change all their leadership, or in another extreme, a school could be forced to close. There were several critics of NCLB. The Obama administration ended No Child Left Behind in 2015 and introduced the Every Student Succeed Act (ESSA).

Every Student Succeeds Act (ESSA). While student monitoring introduced with NCLB continued with modification, ESSA introduced new elements that softened the regimented requirements that had resulted in assessment penalties. Instead, ESSA considered the overall health of the school system as it examined more holistic factors associated with student growth. These new factors extended beyond test scores and were better received by the education community. For example, students who do not speak English as their first language were monitored for progress. Plans to help students prepare for college enrollment were inspected and school safety was also identified as a factor in whole student success and health. In addition, ESSA focused on reporting associated with student attendance and linked consequences to high absenteeism. More importantly, generous funds were made available to the schools to help with any of the shortcomings discovered by ESSA activities.

TITLE FUNDS

There are several funds and grants that are made available to aid the success of student learning, but not many are as multi-pronged as the federal government's Title funding for K12 systems. This fund is earmarked for disadvantaged students and students who simply need more assistance to overcome some of the blockers that threaten their academic journey. One of the stipulations that school districts must adhere to is a very high-level monitoring and reporting of how the funds are spent. Depending on the school's ability to demonstrate need and the district's size (or number of students classified as having been or potentially impacted by poverty), this fund can invest several million dollars into a school district within a year.[29]

The Title program, funded by the federal government, aims to support students in low-income communities as a priority. Still, the fund does require various layers of reporting and monitoring as a part of the grant entitlement. Title 1 funding promotes instructional programs, services, and other resources to enrich students' educational experiences and outcomes. Schools that are eligible to receive Title I funding identify students who are at high risk based on social and academic factors and provide them with additional support through the fund. This support can be in the form of additional teachers, tutors, small group instruction, and mentorship programs. It is essential and beneficial for parents to be aware that these funds exist and learn about the specific services their child is eligible to receive, the benefits for their families, and how to benefit from them.

For parents who have an assumption or know that their child requires a bit of extra support through a tutor or other resources, Title funds may offer the tutoring services needed without out-of-pocket funding from the family. For this reason, some parents who have children with special needs may choose to move their child from a private school setting with fewer funds to meet the family's needs in a public

---

29   NCES, (2024).

school that receives far more special funding. The path to obtaining these resources starts with basic questions. "Is this a title school? My child needs "i.e., a tutor, special instruction for …" "Can you help?" It is important to stress and ask for what your child needs even if the school is not associated with grant funding. There may be someone who can help secure your child the additional resources desired to help them bridge gaps. Do not be a parent who does not advocate for their child within a school system because of an incorrect belief that all educators are too busy or detached to help. On the contrary, many teachers and administrators were still called and gifted to lead and support children in their academic efforts. Step forward to partner with the school system; there will likely be someone there to welcome you.

ENGLISH LANGUAGE LEARNERS / ENGLISH AS A SECOND LANGUAGE

Student populations within K12 settings reflect the United States as a diverse nation. School districts are required by federal law to support students whose primary language is anything other than English. In the fall of 2020, English learners were recorded as being 10 percent of the population in 12 states. In Texas, English learners, according to one study, were 20.1 percent of the student population.[30] Teachers who set elevated expectations for these learners and instill a belief that learning is possible have been more influential in the successful teaching of this population. After-school activities that reinforce learning that has occurred in the schools can be just the extra time needed to immerse students in more learning. (ref: Winning Schools for ELL). The Title III fund specifically aims to provide additional resources to these populations. As a parent of a child attending these schools, you can find out how these funds are spent each year and if resources are available to help individual students and families.

---

30   National Center for Education Statistics, (2024).

There are 9 Titles in ESSA:[31]

TITLE I: Improving Basic Programs Operated by State and Local Education Agencies (tutors, special instructors, transportation, etc.)

TITLE II: Preparing, Training, and Recruiting High-Quality Teachers, Principals, or Other School Leaders

TITLE III: Language Instruction for English Learners and Immigrant Students

TITLE IV: 21st-Century Schools

TITLE V: State Innovation and Local Flexibility

TITLE VI: Indian, Native Hawaiian, and Alaska Native Education

TITLE VII: Impact Aid

TITLE VIII: General Provisions

TITLE IX: Education for the Homeless and Other Law

Finally, parents should also know that very transparent accountability measures are tied to how Title funds are spent within schools. The U.S. Department of Education monitors the implementation and progress of Title programs by receiving ongoing reporting feedback from school districts. to ensure compliance with federal regulations and to confirm effective implementation. Parents can review their local education agency or state department of education for information and resources related to Title investments. Most state departments of education list Title information on their websites for easy access to such reports. Try googling "your state's name," followed by the Department of Education, to find the main government website. Thousands of dollars are invested in schools each year that are earmarked for helping students and families in need. Knowing how this money is being spent, a parent is prepared to discuss what might

---

31   National Association of Secondary School Principals, (n.d.).

be available for their child's needs that the school system might have innocently overlooked.

LOCAL POLICY (WRITTEN AND MONITORED BY THE SCHOOL DISTRICT)

School divisions draft their local policies that govern their schools only. Some of these policies are directly influenced by federal legislation, while others may be specific to the individual district's needs. The list below contains a few of the local policies likely within your school district. When searching for these policies on your school district's website or calling the school's administrative assistant, please ask for the policy by name or for the policy that might contain what you need.

ATTENDANCE POLICY

An attendance policy aims to promote consistent student attendance, reduced absences, more class attendance, and increased learning opportunities

Schools have an attendance policy or similar language in other school-wide policies that address chronic absenteeism. Chronic absenteeism has been defined in many ways, but most reference approximately "15" missed days in a school year to be tagged as chronic absenteeism. For parents, knowing how many absences are referenced in the school's attendance policy is vital because chronic absenteeism can trigger major consequences. Chronic absenteeism is a federal marker, meaning that these numbers impact school district review and funding.

Each school's policy varies. There can be several attempts to communicate with the family, attempts to meet at the school physically, or external committee interventions to address the reason for student absences. Parents can even face costly fines or jail time for their child's repeated absences in some states. Not only can parents be fined, but students can also lose the opportunity to pass their grades or graduate on time. This occurs when some school policies specify that students can be disqualified for graduation or grade promotion if they miss a specified number of school days. This is due to seat time requirements, which are a part of the graduate profile. All high school graduates must have a specified number of school hours to be eligible for graduation. In other words, a student could have straight As but have too many absences and be at risk of not graduating.

TIPS TO GUIDE YOU IN REVIEWING THE ATTENDANCE POLICY

You will want to look for the following as you scan the policy:

- Common Definitions to Know
- Expected Communications (both parent and school system) and Escalation Path
- Consequences

COMMON DEFINITIONS TO KNOW

CLASSIFICATIONS OF ABSENCES:

a. **Excused Absences**: Absences that can be either pre-approved or approved by the school administration as valid causes for absence, such as illness, doctors' appointments, or immediate family bereavement. These absences may require a note from the parent and an artifact (i.e., doctor's note, obituary, etc.) if the maximum days for excused and acceptable absences are exceeded.

b. **Unexcused Absences**: Absences for which a parent or guardian has not provided adequate explanation/documentation or has not been approved.

c. **Truancy**: Unexcused absence(s) or excessive lateness for all or part of the school day that are numerous in quantity. The attendance policy will specify the number of absences considered "truancy."

EXPECTED COMMUNICATION AND ACTIONS

a. **Parental Notification**: Parents or guardians must notify the school office on the day of absence or provide advance notice explaining the reason for the absence. Proper documentation is required within the stipulated time frame.

b. **Extended Absences**:If a student will be absent for more than" X" consecutive days, the parents or guardians must notify the school administration in advance, provide a reason for the absence, and project a return date. The school will specify the number of days that define an extended period within the policy.

c. **Make-Up Work**: Some school policies will provide students with recommendations on how to seek makeup work while away. If a "makeup" clause does not exist in the policy, it is the student's responsibility to contact their teachers to get missed assignments and request permission to participate in any tests that occurred during the absences. It is not the teacher's responsibility to provide the student with missed assignments, so be certain to ask your student to request work missed on such occasions if it occurs. Schools are required to allow students to make up work missed during an absence, but there are often time restraints on how long students have to turn these assessments in.

CONSEQUENCES

a. Excused Absences: There will likely be no consequences applied for valid excused absences; however, there may be an associated number of excused absences that will not meet the minimum required days in school for graduation or promotion. It is important to understand this number and know if the minimum number of school days to graduate is mentioned in the policy. For instance, if the student attends a class for three months, your child has missed school

UNEXCUSED ABSENCES:

1. Students with "x" or more unexcused absences may face disciplinary actions, including detention (which results in missed days in school - - which has its own consequences of missed instruction), attendance improvement plans, and parental meetings.

2. Excessive unexcused absences may result in class failure, loss of academic credit, retention, or even legal consequences for families.

TRUANCY:

1. Students found to be truant may face disciplinary actions, including detention, required parental meetings, or even suspension, depending on the number of days involved.

2. Continued truancy may result in loss of credit, retention, or legal interventions.

TECHNOLOGY POLICY

Purpose: Overview of digital citizenship and its importance in K12 education

Technology use has become commonplace in most school districts and classrooms. Yet, with all the benefits associated with technology and learning (and there are many), new liabilities have been introduced due to technology use. Schools protect themselves and their students by crafting well-thought rules and guidelines in the form of technology policy and procedure.

Acceptable Use, Technology, or Internet Use Policy

Schools adopt policies that govern expected student behavior when accessing the internet in school and often outside of school boundaries. These policies address internet access for laptops and computers and/or mobile device use. Depending on the school's discretion, there could be many categories within an internet policy, but let us highlight a few definitions. We will also visit why knowing these definitions is important to parents.

Let's get right down to it -- **not** knowing the policy for your child's school can result in undesirable consequences such as in-school suspension, automatic semester failure, restitution, and even expulsion. Some districts require parents to review and sign the school's technology and acceptable use policy. The technology policy contains terms that address acceptable and unacceptable hardware and software practices. School districts require parental review of the technology policy to ensure both the parent and child are aware of the school's expectations of use. Parental signature for the use of the school's technology is not unusual, given the larger investments that school districts make in both hardware and software. Laptops can be costly, as can be the applications that are used for learning.

The policy is usually found on the school district's website. If not found on the website, this one is worth a phone call to the school's executive assistant. Ask where you might find a copy of the school's internet use policy. Remember, there are some strict consequences for failure to adhere to this policy and unfortunately multiple students fall into the pitfall of not knowing the rule or not knowing how easily they could be caught breaking the rule. Now, let's explore a few parts that might be found in a technology policy and highlight some of the protections that are found in each.

Parental Consent

To protect themselves and students, school districts will require parental review of the technology acceptable use plan. Since so much of education now revolves around online learning but exposure to other information on the internet and the often pricey technology hardware used.

Hardware Use

There can be a clause that instructs students to take special care with the computer and printer equipment used in the school or taken home. Vandalism is prohibited and such acts usually come with consequences. As a precautionary measure (and to separate the student from any appearance of involvement in device harm), students that have not harmed a device must beware of unfounded associations. For example, if a student is in a classroom where assets are shared and a damaged device is distributed for the class period, that student should quickly make the teacher aware. This will reduce the possibility of blame association.

Software

Standard Software - Devices that belong to the school system generally have software installed prior to distribution. The policy will usually contain a language warning against attempting to install other software. In most cases, the device will contain software that will prevent any attempts to install new software without the user having special or administrative rights to do so. Even then, there are always ways to circumvent controls. *Students should not install any new software onto the device unless instructed by a teacher in writing or in a classroom setting.* Software like spyware, key-loggers, etc., will be prohibited as this software is associated with malicious intent.

Password sharing – Even if not in the policy, students should never share passwords. Here is why... This is one of the only ways a student can prove that he or she did not perform a prohibited behavior while using a school device. If a student openly shares their password, and user IDs within the school, another student meaning harm could do something on a device that the student would later be blamed for. Secondly, students should use strong passwords, something that is not easily guessed. Lastly, when logging into a device, students should consider typing quickly or take special care that no one is watching to learn their passwords and later use them. Not surprisingly, children in K12 can be friends one day and angry at each other the next. On one of those "angry" days, your student wants to be protected from possible retaliations that could originate because of an unrequired share of a password. While *your* child might not do something so harmful, there may be another student who will. Remember there are consequences to this intentional behavior. As parents, we want to make certain consequences are not a surprise for children.

Cyberbullying

Bullying in any form is wrong and can be devastating for the children that are targeted. Students that are bullied can suffer emotional impact, feelings of isolation, and academic impact as well as other negative impacts. In 2010, the Department of Education introduced bullying guidelines that could be adopted into school policies. States had the opportunity to personalize their own methods of bullying policy delivery. To review your states anti-bullying laws and policies visit (1.) Your state's Department of Education website (2.) Website- https://www.stopbullying.gov/resources/laws. At the time of this publication this site has an easy to follow United States map that will show the guidelines for each state when clicked. If your student is the one being bullied or is the one doing the bullying, parents should know that schools are required to report and respond to allegations in this area.

Communications

Email Message – Schools have made provisions to protect students by using software that proactively manages email use. Emails within many public schools are not private and are routinely scanned and reported upon. Content management software usually scans these emails to identify and classify user types. For instance, computer scanning software can be programmed to identify profane language, racism, violent behavior associations (guns, fights, stabs), drug names, and references to sexual preference. In addition, filters can be set up to block and generate reports that pinpoint the Login ID or computer name associated with reported behavior. Even though the filter can block content from being sent to its intended recipient, some content scanners capture attempted communications in shareable reports that will identify the origin. Therefore, students can be held accountable if an unacceptable email reaches its intended destination.

Please consider instructing your students to avoid typing correspondence when they have experienced something that has angered or disappointed them. Remember to remain polite and avoid profanity and any form of bullying.

File Storage – Downloads, file saves, distributions.

Social Media

Each school district has its own guidelines of what a student and teacher can and cannot do online. For students, physical harm threats, bullying, and pornography are a short list of when social media use can be detrimental to reputations and student well-being.

Few students do not post or enjoy the world of social media. Responsible social media use means being conscious of the content we share online and its infinite lifespan. It is important to think before posting anything, pictures or worse, online. Once "enter" is pressed, it is unlikely that a student can retract contact or the associated history. Be respectful of others when posting comments or sharing content, and always consider the potential impact of your words and actions on others.

Years ago, some young students explored the human body, peeping at nude magazines. Their parents may have scolded and taught them a verbal lesson, but times have changed. This is a big lesson for parents to learn. Peeping **and** saving on social media can mean jail time!!! Yes, you read it right, Jail Time! Students as young as 12 have been charged with juvenile offenses in the judicial system, found guilty, and required to spend time in juvenile jail systems. This happens not only because a student downloads or takes a picture of nudity or partial nudity online but more commonly because the subject of the picture is underage. A student does not even have to be the one who captures the image. Still, if it can be proven that your student has such a photo on their computer, laptop, or phone, they could be associated with a criminal offense (child pornography).

This publication is not intended to provide legal advice. Still, please make your students aware that if that beautiful young man or woman that they have met in school (who is so likely a teenager or below) shares a nude picture with them. If they are caught with such a photograph, there could be severe legal consequences. Encourage them to tell you if this occurs so that you can seek proper guidance. Not having such a photo in one's possession or posting such a photo on social media may be the best choice to avoid such situations. This is a heartfelt recommendation. Parents and students are devastated each school year because this lesson is found out the hard way, without expectation of the grave consequences.

Content Filter Systems (Use)

We hope to always do what is right but if you know you are being watched it's even more wise not to fall into wrongdoing. Here is what is important to know about one of the school systems internet and laptop monitoring tools and its origin. In 2000,

Congress adopted the Child Internet Protection Act (CIPA) to protect children from harmful internet content.[32] CIPA attached the requirement for schools to purchase a content filter that would reduce the dangers of student internet use by filtering or blocking bad content. To further encourage participation, Congress tied the requirement of purchasing a content filter to federal approval of school grants such as E-rate.[33] In short, if schools wanted to continue to receive generous technology grants using a content filter had become a prerequisite.

Content filtering systems are software applications installed on a computer/laptop, or more modern devices are connected to the internet. The primary job of a Content system is to track and log internet activity for a device. Tracking student and staff activity is commonplace inside school walls and is equally common when using school devices outside school boundaries. Not only do these applications track activity, but depending on their configuration, they are set up to block inappropriate, objectionable, and illegal internet access.

Most content filtering systems can be configured, for instance, to block specific websites and scan others based on scan returns for items such as gambling or pornography. Bullying or profanity. No child or parent should be surprised that the "School walls (the internet) have ears AND "Big Brother IS watching." These controls are intended to protect children from content that is not age-appropriate and just vile. Yet, no content filter can catch or monitor everything.

Many students have landed in the principal's office, met with a written log containing visits to inappropriate sites or a log that shows the number of times the content filter blocked attempts to access an inappropriate website. The consequences could be as simple as a warning or far more severe. The school policy

---

32   Consumer Guide: Children's Internet Protection Act (CIPA), (2000).
33   Congress.gov. S.97, (2024).

should outline expectations. Here is the warning – make certain your child is neither surprised nor embarrassed to discover that their school related internet access is monitored.

Content Filter (Limitations)

Content Filters do block websites from access if preliminary scans of a website suggest inappropriate content. Never-the-less, there are occasions where the filter may falsely block educational content that is, in fact, appropriate and times when the filter will, in contrast, "miss" and allow inappropriate content to be seen. When these occasions occur, Content filtering systems can be configured to consider White- and Blacklist. The "Whitelist" contains predefined URL addresses for websites that have proven to be appropriate while the Blacklist contains URLs that might have been missed by the automated filter but have been identified to contain inappropriate content. Both the White and Blacklist can be modified.

Protecting Your Child's Digital Reputation

Digital Footprint and Reputation Management: K-12 students need to be aware of the concept of a digital footprint - the trail of information they leave behind online. Understanding how their online activities can impact opportunities, such as college admissions and job applications is essential. Teaching students how to understand their role in protecting their digital footprint is a critical aspect of digital citizenship education. Unfortunately, students can be the target of information as well. This makes PII for teens very desirable by those that have malicious intent to gain access and reuse their information.[34] Sharing too much can attract online thieves who seek to steal student identities for personal gain such as credit card schemes and the like. Students should practice guarding their personal identifiable information (PII) as a part of their digital behavior. An example of some information sharing that students should avoid where possible:

---

34   U.S Department of Education, (2024).

Social Security Number

Address

Middle Name

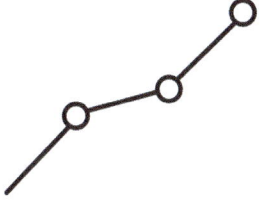

CHAPTER 6

GUIDED GROWTH CAPTURING THE ADVANTAGES OF ASSESSMENT

Few students would stand in line to take a test if it were not a requirement; Testing is just not something most people find enjoyable. Despite the unpopularity of testing, there is value associated with using the results of a test to inform teaching and learning needs. Testing students, both the types of tests given and their frequency, is controversial. Various test and assessment types are available to educators, and usually, school districts select multiple types to administer throughout the school year. The federal and state governments can mandate assessments. Some tests can be used to determine if a student will be promoted from one grade level to another. Other test scores can determine if a student qualifies to be placed in advanced classes. There are also assessments that compare a student's performance to other students.

Let's explore a few words associated with formal ways student academic progress is communicated:

Assessments – In general, these are tests given to students, and the results are used to gauge a student's mastery or learning level in subject areas. While there are many types of assessments, there are two main differences that characterize testing in K12: (1.) The time when the tests are administered, i.e., beginning of the year, mid-year, end of the year. (2.) The standard to which test scores are being compared to determine if a student is below, at, or beyond the expected. Some of the baseline types are associated with federal or local requirements, and baselines can be established, in part, based on factors researched by the testing companies. Three more commonly used tests are formative assessments, summative assessments, and benchmarks.

ALL GRADES

Formative Assessments_- These tests are administered at the beginning and throughout the year but are rarely administered at the end of the year. The results will inform teachers, principals, and districts of student progress. While there may be many associated reports related to test results, the results tell the reader if a student is below, at, or above the aptitude expected for the subject and grade level. Teachers can opt to use assessment results to guide how extra time in a subject area might benefit a student's progress, whether this is additional time spent with the entire class, guided by large percentages of the class having a deficiency in an area, or with individual students to pull their learning to where it is expected for the school year.

Why are assessments necessary for parents? Report card content and end-of-year grades should never surprise the parent or student. Reviewing formative assessments, parents obtain up-to-date information on their child's academic progress and can:

Request targeted assistance from the teacher or school to assist their child in moving to or beyond grade-level understanding. If you are not receiving the results of your child's assessments, ask for them. Ask for the planned date of assessments so that you can make certain to place these dates or a range of dates on your calendar. Help your child by making certain they are reminded to rest the night before so that they will be at their best and alert. Once the assessments are completed and analyzed, you may want to review the results and determine if your student is being classified as at, *below, or above* in a subject and ask for assistance as needed. Assistance can come in many forms. Here are a few:

- The teacher may choose to give the student slightly more homework in the areas of trouble. In doing so, the teacher will be able to analyze the current issue and offer guidance to change course as the homework is reviewed.
- Schools often have tutors available in the evenings or during specified periods of the school day. If your child has not been offered a tutor, parents can advocate for their child by requesting additional assistance from the school.
- Identify an online tool that can be used at home that teaches the subject area. In doing so, the child can spend time outside of the classroom focusing on the area of deficiency and elevating their level of mastery in the subject area.

Benchmark Assessments - These assessments are like formative assessments. Benchmark tests are usually administered at the beginning or far before the end of the year. Just as a formative assessment, benchmarks should be administered in time to improve a lower classification or grade by seeking an intervention step for the student to achieve grade-level status with applications of additional work/intervention. One of the primary differences between formative assessments and benchmarks is that the benchmark test will provide reports that can compare the performance of students in the same classroom and students in the same subject in other classrooms. These reports can be used to determine if an entire classroom is underperforming over time. In such cases, there may be an adjustment in instruction needed, or there might be a need to investigate the strengths of the students entering the classroom at the beginning of the semester. This type of information, if studied, may inform school districts in investigating areas that may be contributing to weaker performance.

Summative Assessments - These assessments are usually performed at the end of the year. For school districts who must report the progress of their district to state and federal governance organizations, the results of these test can determine additional funding amounts for schools through grants, school rankings used to attract (or warn) parents about districts based on performance and influence the classes that are assigned to a student in the coming school year.

I believe summative assessments are a bit less important than formative assessments. These results are final. When summative assessments are administered, there is little time to make changes for the purposes of final grades. Summative assessments are a final "snapshot" of how well a student has done in the final semester or school year. One of the advantages of a summative assessment is that any deficiencies can be addressed during the summer (if it is an end of year assessment.) The advice here is to make efforts to improve, where needed, prior to the time of summative assessment.

REPORT CARDS

School districts have different periods to release report cards to students and parents. These dates are usually found on the school's website. Depending on the school district, report cards may be mailed, some printed and given directly to the students, and other times, report cards are made available digitally. As a parent, you will want to know when report cards will be available. If your student loses theirs on the way home, parents need to know when to ask for a copy to be reprinted or sent to them electronically. Interim report cards are a time for parents to learn how their student is performing, to again ask questions if the performance is not what is expected and work with the school system to identify ways to assist your student in intervention should such actions be necessary. Final report cards (end of semester or end of year) leave little to no movement for change.

This is why it is crucial to seek and review interim grades for your student regularly. Make it a part of your routine review year by year.

There may be an occasion when there is a disconnect between the grades your students receive in a classroom report card and the feedback from an assessment. There could be multiple explanations for such discrepancies. For instance, a teacher's grading can be subjective. Assessment feedback ranges are usually based on the provider's scale of where it is thought a student should be in aptitude at a particular time of the year or grade. One of the reasons this might require a conversation with your student's teacher is that some assessments can be classified as "high stakes." High-stakes assessments can determine if a student is promoted from one grade to another or if a student graduates. If there is an assessment that reveals your student is below an expected level, but the student is receiving good grades in a classroom subject, it may be prudent to review what areas in the subject the assessment has identified as weaker. In doing so, you and the teacher can work together to see if there could be a plan to strengthen those deficient areas. This is important because some weaknesses grow stronger as the grade level and impact increase.

HIGH SCHOOL ONLY

Scholastic Aptitude Test (SAT) – The SAT test is one of several assessments that some colleges use to determine who will be accepted into their schools. When participating in this test, a part of the process is for students to identify which schools with which results will be shared. High schools have several dates on which the SAT can be taken. In fact, students can take the SAT test as many times as they would like. The College Board recommends taking the test one time in the Spring of Junior (11th grade) year and again in the fall of senior year (12th grade).[35] The PSAT is also offered to Sophomores (10th grade) in order for students to experience the test

---

[35] Satsuite.collegeboard.org, (2024).

prior to their 11th/12th grade years. These PSAT scores are also used by school counselors to gauge the successful placement of students into advanced courses.

College Level Examination Program (CLEP) – These tests are used to gain college course credit at a fraction of the cost of enrolling in a class. Using this route, families may be able to save money towards college and students can use these credits to finish college earlier. The one caveat is that students can be very burnt out in their junior and senior year of school and taking another test might not be on their lists of "excited to do," If saving money is a goal (and it's a goal for almost everyone) if your student is willing to pursue taking this test, there may be much benefit.

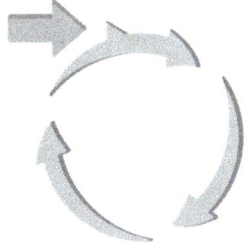

INTERVENTIONS (CATCHING UP AND SURPASSING EXPECTATIONS)

Specialized academic support programs play a crucial role in helping students falling behind catch up and excel academically. These programs provide individualized attention and guidance that can significantly impact a student's learning journey. In this section, we will highlight the importance of various programs, including one-on-one tutoring, peer tutoring, volunteer tutoring, group teaching, professional tutoring, individualized education plans, and technology resources.

One-on-one tutoring offers assistance tailored to the specific needs of an individual student. This level of individualized support enables tutors to improve the likelihood of identifying a student's strengths and weaknesses, address gaps in knowledge, and develop strategic plans for improvement. For instance, some students may struggle with a particular subject, while others may require assistance with learning to study or time management. One-on-one tutoring allows for a customized approach to address these unique challenges, hoping to improve academic performance as a return on time investment. The obstacle to obtaining one-on-one time for a child may be the sheer number of students that are in the regular classroom. Remember, if a parent is seeking one-on-one tutoring from a teacher, a teacher in middle school (for example) may see over 100 students per day. Consider that if 80% of those students are behind, it is unlikely that each student will receive one-on-one tutoring from their teacher. If a parent is seeking one-to-one tutoring for their student, consider the following:

- Advocate for your child in a private setting with the teacher. There may be times when a request in solitude will result in a yes while a request within a crowd may not be as favorable.
- Be open to having someone other than the teacher tutor your student. It is more than appropriate to ask for the background of the teacher. For instance, if your student is in elementary school, asking if the tutor has experience with elementary students in the subject of need is perfectly suitable. While not completely within the topic, whenever giving permission for your student to meet with someone outside of regular school hours, the general advice is to ask enough questions to feel that your student will be safe especially if your student is in elementary years or below.
- **Peer tutoring** is a type of tutoring program where students who are academically stronger help other students to learn. This approach fosters a supportive and collaborative learning environment usually within the same classroom. Peer tutors can relate to the struggles of their peers and offer guidance based on their own learning styles. This type of tutoring can not only enhance academic skills but also build confidence and promote social interaction among students. Thus, the results of using peer tutoring can be twofold: (1.) Academic Improvement (2.) Social Connection. Also, since peer tutoring is often orchestrated within the same learning environment, peer tutoring reduces feelings of being singled out or embarrassed. If a student does not understand a concept or falls behind, sometimes a student simply needs a concept to be explained in another way to grasp the concept.

Chapter 7: Interventions (Catching Up and Surpassing Expectations)

Peer tutoring allows this opportunity. Not all teachers utilize this intervention style in their classrooms, but teachers may be open to the suggestion of adding this intervention type if requested. This is not a new intervention type by any means, but one that can be very effective in reaching students who are too shy to ask for help in the larger one-to-many classroom format.

Volunteer tutoring programs involve volunteers from the community who give their time and expertise to support students. This type of tutoring can provide additional resources to schools that may have limited funding or human resources available to perform in additional staff roles. Volunteer tutors can assist students with homework, provide guidance on assignments, and reinforce learning concepts. The very existence of volunteers in a school can also contribute to more use of one-to-one tutoring opportunities. By giving back to the community, these tutors also model the practice of meaningful community involvement to students. The academic and social backgrounds of volunteers can vary, which may impact their effectiveness, but this is also true with any other instructional leader. As a note, volunteers are generally required to pass some level of background check prior to tutoring a student or group of students. The level of background check will vary by school, but such checks might include:

(1) Confirmation that the volunteer is not included in the sex offender registry.

(2) Confirmation that there has not been a recent criminal offense.

(3) Confirmation that there has been no history of child abuse or negligence.

Schools can opt to use school visitor management software that performs levels of these checks based on fingerprints or personally identifiable information (PII) such as social security numbers. Some school visitor management software systems have a feature that will allow the system to take and store pictures of visitors within the database. At the time of this publication, vendors such as Raptor,

Verkada and Visitu are a few examples of companies that compete and sell to school systems to perform these functions. These systems, if used, may be located at any point within the school, but the main office is usually a convenient location. When you visit your student's school, you may encounter visitor management software as you sign in, or your electronic signature may be requested in such a system for school entry.

Group teaching is another form of intervention where a tutor works with a small group of students. This approach also allows for shared learning experiences and peer collaboration. This intervention can be preferred for several reasons. Group teaching can be attractive for students who prefer a more interactive learning environment because the teacher has more time to attend to learning challenges. Group teaching can include ***differentiated*** learning. Differentiated learning allows students to learn concepts that are geared toward their individual needs. For instance, there may be a set of students on one side of the classroom who are studying double-digit multiplication problems because they have mastered single digits while the other side of the class works toward single-digit mastery. Another possible advantage of this approach can be more cost-saving for schools because a single teacher or tutor is able to affect several students in a single setting.

PROFESSIONAL TUTORS

Lastly, professional tutoring services offer specialized support for students who require intensive academic assistance. These tutors often hold advanced degrees or certifications in specific subjects and are trained to work with complex learning needs. Unfortunately, one of the drawbacks for parents as it pertains to professional tutoring services can be cost. Not all schools nor parents can afford professional tutors outside of school, but thankfully, there are other alternatives. Local college students are usually easily found by contacting the college to see what students may be available and in what subject matter. Also, online applications like Upwork and Fiverr allow parents to search a database of tutors and their qualifications to determine if one is the best fit for their student. Cost will vary but this provides parents with a possible option. It's important to somehow gauge the prospective tutor's effectiveness. Since this relationship with your student should be online, there is a level of safety, but I would still monitor such relationships for my student in K12.

In conclusion, academic support programs are vital for students who are falling behind or even want to get ahead. These programs provide personalized focus, address individual shortcomings, and offer strategies for improvement. Whether through peer tutoring, volunteer tutoring, group teaching, or professional tutoring services, the availability of different types of tutoring programs ensures that students have access to the support they need to succeed academically.

Tutoring and academic support programs play a crucial role in helping students who are falling behind catch up and excel academically. These programs provide individualized attention and guidance that can make a significant difference in a student's learning journey.

TECHNOLOGY-BASED INTERVENTIONS

Technology plays a crucial role in supporting struggling students and providing them with computer applications that can adjust to the student's personalized learning needs in order to guide remediation. These types of applications that adjust in complexity to learn the strengths and weaknesses of a child in a content area are usually referenced as "Adaptive" software. Educational software, online learning platforms, and assistive technology devices have significantly enhanced the reach of educators by adjusting teaching delivery styles to many students in ways that a single teacher could not reach such large numbers, each with customized learning delivery. These technological tools provide targeted interventions, adaptive learning experiences, and increased accessibility, ultimately empowering struggling students to succeed.

Various software programs exist that address specific subject areas and skills. For example, software programs are dedicated to improving reading comprehension, mathematical concepts, and even literary skills. These programs often use interactive and engaging methods to present material, making the learning experience more enjoyable yet effective for students as a reliable intervention choice. Online learning platforms have also proven invaluable in supporting struggling students. These platforms offer a wide range of courses and resources that cater to various learning needs and styles. Students can access these platforms at their own pace, allowing them to revisit concepts as necessary and work through materials at a comfortable speed. Additionally, online learning platforms often incorporate features such as progress tracking and instant feedback, enabling students to monitor their own growth and receive immediate guidance when needed.

Schools often provide online learning platforms to students to allow the learning experience beyond the confinement of schools. If a school is not doing so, ask if this could be a consideration but also plan to invest in such software to enhance your child's learning options without delay. To help in your choice, ask your child if there are programs used at school that they find helpful and might be beneficial **to use at** home. If there is not a particular software that is used, scan the internet to search for software that addresses your child's needs. Before the purchase, look for reviews that might reveal testimonies that detail the effectiveness of the software tool considered.

Assistive technology, both hardware and software, is widely used to assist students with different types of disabilities. This software, for instance, can be essential in providing students with special needs the necessary accommodations and support that mainstream software and instruction do not. For example, students with visual impairments can utilize screen reading software and speech-to-text tools. Students with attention deficit disorders may benefit from technology as basic as noise-canceling headphones, which aid them in their ability to remain focused even in larger class settings. Ear sanitization may be a concern. To combat this, some schools utilize sanitizer wipes or plastic overlays for the earpiece between classroom use. Such devices and software not only level the playing field for more students to learn but also empower students to overcome what could have been a larger block to reaching their full potential.

In addition to tailored learning experiences, educational software applications also offer teachers useful data and insights into student performance. Through data analytics, educators can monitor areas of weakness, track progress, and adjust instruction accordingly to provide timely direction to students. This data-driven approach enables teachers to individualize their teaching methods and foster improved educational outcomes for students who were once struggling to learn.

INDIVIDUALIZED EDUCATION PLANS (IEP)

Individualized education plans (IEPs) are specifically tailored plans designed to meet the unique needs of students who are struggling academically. These plans ensure that students with learning impediments, special needs, or other academic challenges receive the necessary support and accommodations to help them improve in school. The creation of an IEP involves a collaborative process between parents, teachers, and specialists to identify the student's individual learning objectives and establish appropriate strategies to meet those objectives.

The process of creating an IEP begins with the identification of a student's learning challenges. This could be initiated by a teacher or parent who notices persistent difficulties in the student's academic performance and behaviors that indicate a potential learning disability. This could include issues such as trauma, depression, low self-esteem, anxiety, or difficulties with social interactions. Communicate with your child often. Talk to your child about their feelings and experiences so that if there are underlying experiences that may be impacting them academically, those can surface, and your student has the potential to receive specialized attention to help them perform better. Remember, you do not have to be an expert in all things K12 to remain engaged in the practical steps of offering love, support, and encouragement as your child does the work to progress in their academic pursuit. Never underestimate the support of you, the parent, in motivating students to press forward.

Once a concern is identified, the teacher or parents can request an evaluation of the student's learning needs. Be sure to share any relevant information that you think might be impacting your child's emotional well-being or academic progress. The evaluation is typically conducted by a team of professionals that may include psychologists or other experts in the field. This evaluation helps to identify the specific areas in which the student struggles academically, as well as their emotional strengths, weaknesses, and needs. The team may assess the student's cognitive abilities, educational performance, and any related health or developmental concerns.

Once the evaluation is complete, the team meets to determine eligibility for special education services and to develop the IEP. This meeting, often called the IEP meeting, includes the student's parents or guardians, teachers, specialists, and any other relevant school personnel. The purpose of the IEP meeting is to discuss the findings of the evaluation and collaboratively develop an individualized plan to address the student's needs. During the IEP meeting, participants review the evaluation results, identify the student's strengths and weaknesses, and develop specific goals the students should target. Then, measurable goals are set. These goals often focus on academic performance, social skills, behavior management, and other specific areas of need.

In addition to goals, the IEP includes a description of the modifications, accommodations, and specialized instruction that will be provided to support the student's learning. This may include allocating additional time on assignments or tests, specialized teaching methods, assistive technology, additional support from specialists, or other interventions tailored to the student's needs.

Regarding collaboration, the input of parents or guardians is crucial when developing an IEP. They bring valuable insights into their child's strengths, weaknesses, and learning styles that may not be known fully by the educational system. As follow-ups for students assigned an IEP occur, participants engage in an open dialogue, sharing information and discussing any potential changes to address the student's challenges. In short, the IEP is a negotiated agreement that considers the perspectives of all team members assigned to the student, including the parent. Regularly monitoring the child's progress to ensure interventions are effective is a crucial part of this process. Reassessing the child's socio-emotional development as well as academic progress should be ongoing, and parents should be updated on various points of the process. Parental participation is so important here. If a parent believes that something might help your student, either socially or academically, to progress, make certain that you make those suggestions. This process is a collaborative effort, and the parent's input is key to its success.

Remember, every child is unique, and their individualized support needs can be just as unique. Placing a label of any sort on children is hard to embrace. Labels placed on children such as smart, needing assistance, and SPED are commonly used. Assure your child that labels can come and go and are only temporary, but academic concepts, when learned, can be the unshakeable building blocks that shape their futures.

STUDENTS ASSIGNED IEP

While more detailed discussions should be had with you if your child has been identified as needing an individualized education plan (IEP), a few high-level tasks may help collaborate with schools to assist your student in their personalized plan. As a project management professional, I believe every important meeting should have archived notes that can be referenced. Consider a few steps to assist the school and your student.

STEP I: **Request a copy of your students IEP via email or hardcopy.** If you have an email address, request an electronic copy which can be accessible to you as needed. This plan may include: (a.) A description of the goals set (b.) the timelines for the delivery and targeted result, (3.) the school staff member names and titles included in the plan.

STEP 2: **Plan to take notes at every meeting.** All important meetings have notes that capture, at minimum, what was discussed, existing status of current action items and assignment of new action items. The school will share their notes from the meeting with you if requested. If there are no notes taken, you may consider making a Word template to print out for your meeting that includes: the date, the attendees (name and professional title i.e., Principal, Director of Secondary Education, SPED instructor), plans/goals/timelines discussed, and student progress.

STEP 3: **Ask that Regular Progress Reports of your students' progress be a part of the plan.** Enquire about what type of report you might be receiving and if it will include examples of your child's progress (if applicable).

STUDENTS ASSIGNED IEP

STEP 4: **Ask when the next meeting will occur, if not offered, prior to the meeting's end.** Raise any concerns you might have and request an adjustment of the IEP be considered, if needed. This does not have to occur at a scheduled routine IEP meeting. You might want to arrange a phone conversation with your student's teacher if you have observed something positive or negative that you wish to communicate.

STEP 5: **Familiarize yourself with the Disabilities Education Act (IDEA).** As of September 2024, the website located at the below URL provides information: https://sites.ed.gov/idea/. There are laws, grants, etc. that may be very helpful for you to know as you navigate the possible benefits associated with the IEP process.

CHAPTER 8

COMMUNICATION BLUEPRINTS PARTNERING FOR SUCCESS

This chapter offers practical, general advice on how and when parents should communicate with key school staff. It provides strategies for establishing and maintaining open lines of communication, including regular meetings, email exchanges, phone calls, and parent-teacher conferences, to promote collaboration and support your child's academic and social progress. As we begin this delivery of recommendations, it's important to acknowledge that many parents work **one** or more jobs inside or outside the physical home and then come home to work the "last shift" of that day– taking care of themselves and their children. With this in mind, please know that if you cannot participate in all of the recommendations **but can** do *some* of them, you can still accomplish your goal: Providing your students the emotional and organizational support they need to progress through K12 in a healthy and supportive manner.

Studies have supported the belief that parents who have regular contact with schools are perceived to have high expectations for their children. As a result, teachers may pay more attention to students who have involved parents.[36] This is even more important in an era where some teachers have a "sea" of students in their classrooms. Another benefit is that teachers actually report feeling better about schools and teaching when more parents are involved.[37] As important as the role of the teacher is in the ecosystem of education, teachers too could use a nudge of encouragement in knowing that there is someone who is rooting for a child in their classroom and believes education to be important to their families.

Organizational skills, communication skills, and confidence are some of the many characteristics that are shaped in elementary and middle schools during K12. Especially in elementary school, young students are discovering what it takes to be more organized and learning there is a need to become equipped with mature organizational skills very quickly. Usually, there are test or assignment dates that have been missed (not written down), so even if the student studies without proper organizational skills, their grade point average can quickly diminish during the infancy of their organizational skill development. As younger children develop this skill, it is very beneficial to have a parent that is watching their schedules to help them remain on the proper path. Most teachers distribute course syllabi at the beginning of the school year or semester. In elementary school, receiving a copy to know what will be taught in the class is always a good practice. In many cases teachers will also offer monthly or quarterly calendars to their students that contain dates for reading assignments and sometimes test dates. Young children mature in different time frames, and organizational skill development can be tricky to predict. It may be best for some parents to monitor the information provided by the teacher so that young students, especially, can be reminded of study expectations and important dates.

A. Establish regular meetings: Schedule meetings with key employees to discuss the child's academic performance, behavior,

---

36 Grolnick and Slowiaczek, (1994); Henderson and Berla, (1997).
37 Epstein and Van Voorhis, (2001).

and concerns. These meetings can be in person or through virtual platforms such as Zoom or Microsoft Teams. Regular meetings create a sense of accountability and allow for timely communication of important information.

B. Utilize email correspondence: Email is a convenient way to communicate with key employees when face-to-face meetings are not possible. Parents can use email to convey concerns, ask for updates, or share relevant information about their child. It is important to be clear and concise in the email and ensure that all necessary parties are copied for transparency. Some teachers and school districts may prefer those communications be placed inside of their school online portal because of the uniformity the tools offer. Whichever means of communication you identify, be sure to let educators know that you are a willing and active participant in your student's academic progress.

C. Attend Parent-Teacher Conferences: Parent-Teacher conferences are a formal setting where parents can meet with key employees to discuss their child's progress. These conferences provide an opportunity for a thorough discussion of academic performance, areas for improvement, and strategies for supporting the child's learning at home. Parents should actively participate in these conferences, asking questions and providing insights about their child's needs. Understanding that some parents work more than others, perhaps there is a virtual option at your child's school that will reduce the time needed and bring participation into reach. I can not stress enough that teachers should know your face or voice so that they feel safe and comfortable knowing that you will be willing to receive any needed communication, whether good or bad.

D. Use the school's communication app or platform: Many schools have adopted communication apps or platforms, such as Remind, Class Dojo, or Google Classroom, to facilitate parent-teacher communication. These apps allow for quick updates, reminders, and direct messaging between parents and key employees. Parents should familiarize themselves with the school's chosen platform and utilize it for effective communication.

E. Respect boundaries and be professional: While it is important to establish open lines of communication, it is equally important to respect boundaries. Key employees have multiple responsibilities and may not always be available at a moment's notice. Be respectful of their time and workload. Maintain a professional tone in all interactions. Remember that school employees are partners in educating your students.

As a parent, try to align your schedule with your ability to participate in your students' academic path. As evidenced above, there are many ways to develop your communications plan. Weigh the benefits and your child's needs for each and determine which actions you will include in your arsenal of proactive tools. As you decide, I thought it might be interesting to note the result of a study that compared what teachers and principals' thought would be the best ways for parents to engage versus what parents thought. The study included 1,405 parent and guardian participants, 317 Principals, and 300 teachers. When asked how parents should be involved in the order of precedence, parents believed that (1.) Checking children's assignments at home, (2.) Helping with homework, and (3.) Participating in Parent-teacher Conferences in person were the most important. Teachers agreed with parents in level 1, but in their opinions, their very next belief of importance for parents was communicating regularly with their child's teacher. For principals, their 2nd level belief for parents was that they should visit their child's classroom and provide input on curriculum. This feedback was also captured under the category of "Communicating with Teachers."[38] Without question, schools in the survey identify parent communication with the school and teacher as important to students' success.

---

38   Learning Heroes, (2022).

Here are a few high-level items to know:

School systems have a hierarchy of authority. Though the teacher may be the most impactful and visible resource that a parent interacts with, their authority is limited to certain areas. What hurts so often is to see public communication breakdowns between parents and teachers because of frustration that is often rooted in a misunderstanding of the teacher's level of authority. (Please see image 1. The Educational Hierarchy). Remember, in all interactions, as a parent, even when the conversation is uncomfortable or a bit strained, your desire is to help your student receive what is needed to learn, remain safe, develop socially, and progress through the academic levels. If you are overly aggressive with teachers, you risk not getting what your child needs and ultimately alienating yourself and your child with not only the current teacher but with other teachers. If a conversation with a teacher does not yield a positive result, there is a hierarchy that can be explored to get the opinion or feedback of others within the school system. Doing so positions you as a parent who is advocating for their child in a way that will likely open doors for a more fruitful exchange.

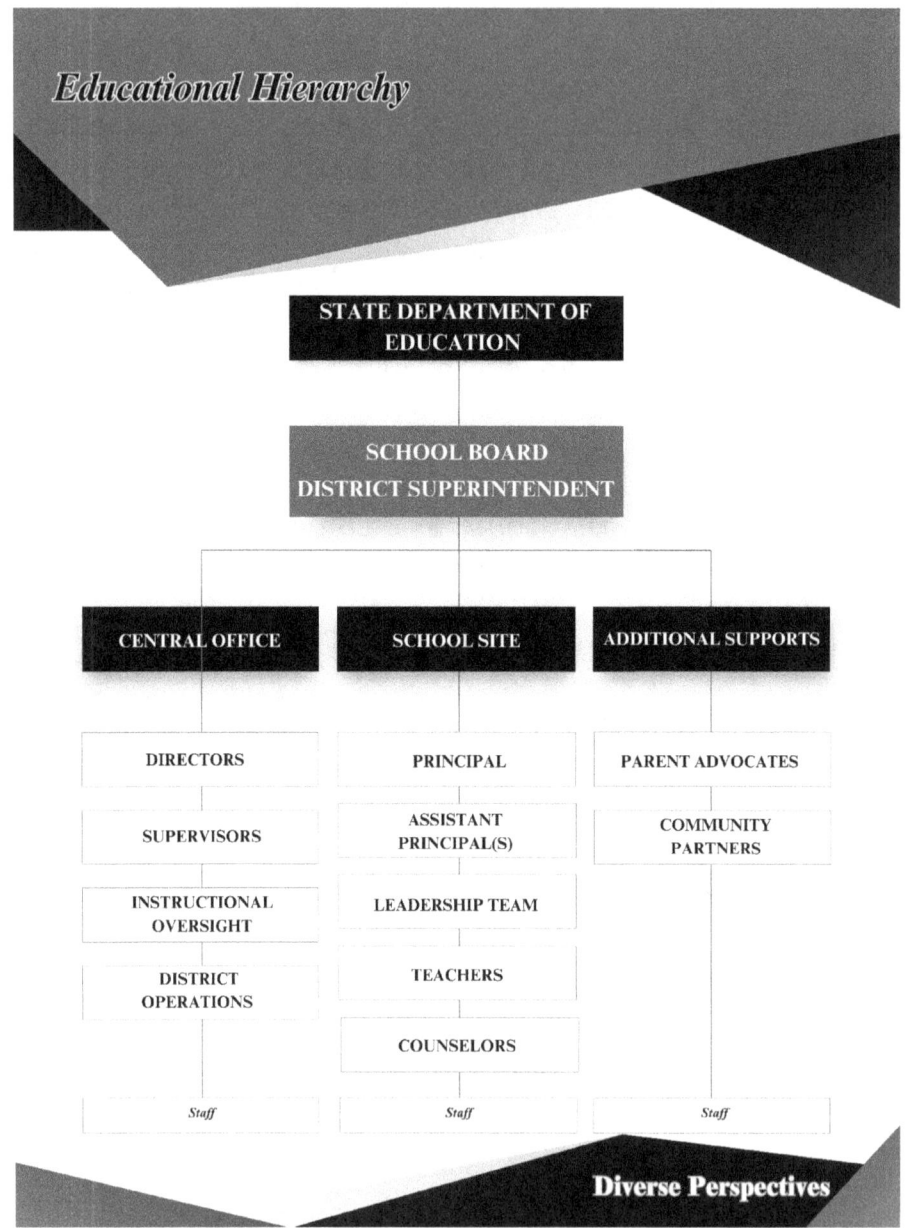

Educational Hierarchy

STATE DEPARTMENT OF EDUCATION

SCHOOL BOARD
DISTRICT SUPERINTENDENT

CENTRAL OFFICE	SCHOOL SITE	ADDITIONAL SUPPORTS
DIRECTORS	PRINCIPAL	PARENT ADVOCATES
SUPERVISORS	ASSISTANT PRINCIPAL(S)	COMMUNITY PARTNERS
INSTRUCTIONAL OVERSIGHT	LEADERSHIP TEAM	
DISTRICT OPERATIONS	TEACHERS	
	COUNSELORS	
Staff	Staff	Staff

Diverse Perspectives

EDUCATIONAL ROLES AND FUNCTIONS

State Department of Education – Executes state and federal law adherence rules and generally provides a large sum of financial support in the form of grant coordination for school districts. **They also determine the federal budget for each school district throughout the state.**

Additional Note: School Budgets are typically comprised of three buckets: Federal, State, & Local Funds. Then there are grant funds.

School Board – Composed of several appointed citizens. These citizens each occupy these positions and represent specific areas within the county or city. The School Board approves the overall school districts budget and has the greatest influence in approving individual school budgets and initiative.

Superintendent – Reports to the School Board. This role is the chief responsible party for all schools associated within the school district.

Central Office – Composed of district leaders that oversee and lead the school division in areas such as Instruction & Curriculum Design, CTE, and School Administration.

Directors of Elementary, Secondary and High School.

School Site –

Principal – Responsible for the school assigned to them. Is accountable for implementing school policy throughout the school. Responsible for the overall operations of a building. **They are also responsible for hiring qualified staff as well as the Instructional and Structural Leaders of their buildings.**

Assistant Principal – Assists the Principal in running the school site. Responsibilities include but are not limited to, discipline, instruction, and departmental oversight. **Also assist in hiring qualified staff and in any other capacity that helps balance the load within the school site.**

School Leadership Team

Administrators (Principal & Assistant Principal(s))

School Counselors

Attendance Officer

School Instructional Leaders (Teachers, Instructional Coaches, etc.)

Teacher – Responsible for classroom teaching, grading, and management. Also responsible for lesson planning, parent communication, non-instructional duties, attending IEP or 504 meetings, and required staff meetings.

Staff

Counselors (School Counselors, Behavioral Counselors, Mental Health Counselors) - Support student's overall success through specialized academic, behavioral, or mental interventions.

Family Liaisons - Help to bridge the gap between the school, parents, and the community.

Attendance Officer - Monitors student attendance and supports families when attendance issues arise.

Administrative Assistants - Maintain the day-to-day of the school office and support administrative needs.

Cafeteria, Janitorial, and Transportation Staff - Make connections and support student well-being daily.

CHAPTER 9

HOME SETTINGS SURROUNDINGS AND BELIEFS THAT SUPPORT LEARNING

As parents, we play a crucial role in fostering our children's organizational skills, which can significantly impact their success in K-12 education. You can help your child develop the skills they need to do their best by providing guidance and creating systems to support organizations. Here are some tips on how to assist your child in developing organizational skills:

1. Set up a dedicated study area: Designate a specific area in your home as a study space for your child. Ensure it is well-lit, has a comfortable chair and desk, and is free from distractions. This area will be a dedicated space for your child to complete their assignments and stay organized. It will also allow you to peep in (depending on the child's age) to track their progress.

2. Establish a routine: Help your child establish a consistent daily routine. Set regular times for doing homework, reviewing

assignments, and preparing for the next school day. A routine will help your child develop a sense of structure and maintain organization in their academic life. Though a set routine or timeframe to start is certainly recommended, as your student ages or matures, begin to offer them the flexibility of selecting times in the evening when they commit to studying.

3. Provide a planner or calendar: Equip your child with a planner or a calendar where they can write down their assignments, deadlines, and upcoming events. Please encourage them to use it diligently, teaching them how to prioritize tasks and manage their time effectively. Even in elementary school, beginning to learn how to manage multiple classrooms is key.

   Suggestion: Let your child be involved in selecting a planner or calendar that suits their preferences. There are various options available, including paper and digital versions. Some children might prefer a physical planner they can carry around, while others might find digital options more convenient. They are more likely to use what they select.

4. Teach prioritization skills: Help your child understand the importance of prioritizing tasks based on urgency and importance. Break down large assignments into smaller, manageable tasks, and teach them how to tackle them systematically. Please encourage them to complete the most crucial tasks first to avoid last-minute rushes. This will help your child to balance play and school activities towards learning the importance of prioritization.

5. Establish a system for organizing materials: Teach your student how to organize their school materials. This can involve using folders, binders, or digital storage systems to categorize and store their assignments, handouts, and notes. A neat and organized system will help them quickly find their needs, reducing stress and wasted time. Consider introducing folders early. Just as in life, teachers appreciate when students go the extra mile to

deliver their assignments without stains and papers without tears and crinkles.

6. When my son was in elementary school, I noticed he would get frustrated trying to find which of his many notebooks, all the same color, was the right one for the class he wanted to study for. There were times when he only brought. We remedied that quickly by purchasing different color notebooks for each subject at the beginning of each school year.

7. Foster independent problem-solving skills: Encourage your child to take ownership of their organizational responsibilities. Instead of immediately providing solutions when they encounter challenges, guide them to brainstorm and find their solutions. Developing problem-solving skills will empower them to manage their tasks and resources efficiently.

8. Be patient and supportive: Developing organizational skills takes time and practice, and not all children adapt to organizational skills at the same rate. Be patient with your child and provide ongoing encouragement and support. Celebrate their successes and help them learn from their mistakes. Remember, every child has a unique learning style and organizational method that works best for them. Adapt these tips to suit your child's needs and preferences. By helping your child develop strong organizational skills, you are equipping them with a valuable tool kit to promote their academic success and lifelong achievements.

9. Create a learning-rich environment: Parents can enhance the home environment by displaying educational posters, maps, and charts, setting up age-appropriate learning puzzles and activities, and providing access to educational games and apps. This creates opportunities for spontaneous learning and keeps children engaged even outside of formal study time. In my son's room, for instance, at a very young age, I had a world map on his closet door and a multiplication chart on his wall. Along with these items, I placed motivational quotes from people I knew he

admired on his walls. I wanted him to always see someone who looked like him excel and overcome any obstacles to success.

10. I really wish I could offer overall home organization skills as an entry here because I firmly believe that your surroundings can influence your overall mood. Raising children, working and going to school made complete organization a bit of a challenge at times; however, I made certain that there was always a place for study in my home that was unobstructed, quiet and ready for use. Whew, I had to be transparent there... Hope this helps!

CHAPTER 10

SCHOOL SAFETY STEERING AWAY FROM KNOWN DANGERS

Each year, parents send their children to school and trust that their children are in safe and nurturing environments. For most students, this perceived safety is closer to reality than others. school can be a safe place, but for others, even their school settings can place them in a threatening position. Parents may not have considered some of the unsafe situations of today over a decade ago, but the dynamics of schools have changed dramatically. With those changes have come differences, and though students have benefited, the advantages have not come without shortcomings.

The purpose of this section certainly is not to "cry wolf," nor scare parents, but to remove any naivety that might surround a few of the topics that are more prevalent than the even news may regularly report. Some events may not be in the news because of the sensitive nature of the incident, or a need to protect the students' identity, and finally, simply because the impact is so widespread and common that it has become commonplace. All in all, though offered in a high-level discussion, it is the hope that after reading this section, parents will identify issues early, assist their children, or, even better, avoid situations with the partnership of their children.

SAFETY ISSUE #1:

RELATIONSHIPS, OPPORTUNITY, AND INAPPROPRIATENESS

The demographic of teachers has changed, and with those changes, students could find themselves in classrooms with teachers who might have been attending the same school as students 2-4 years prior.[39] On many levels, a teacher in proximity in age to the students taught could mean many positives. For instance, teachers who have recently been in the school system as students remember both the positives and negatives they were exposed to and will sometimes use their passion for the educational experience to influence positive change within the student and school system. Also, teachers who have recently graduated from college with education majors will come to the school after being immersed in the most recent studies on how children learn. In having this exposure, these teachers can apply new concepts to reach children who have perhaps been overlooked or under-assisted. In addition, teachers who are closer to the same age as the students usually understand the generational norms and challenges because they are a part of the same era. As parents, our hope is that these advantages would be limitless because of the commonalities that exist between students and teachers. Nevertheless, it must be mentioned that in some cases (though small), there may be an overreaching disadvantage to teachers who are almost the same age as the students they teach – the potential draw of inappropriate sexual or romantic attachments.

---

39   teacherpension.org, (2024).

Some might say, "Some things are better left unsaid." I would suggest that if raising awareness can protect a child, a student, from mental or physical abuse, then the topic should be given light. Similarly, if this chapter can help a parent recognize signs that their child is pursuing or initiating inappropriate attention from a teacher to provide redirection or guidance to their child this conversation is worthy of pursuing. In short, questionable attraction and inappropriate actions can stem from either student or teacher.

This type of misconduct, whether initiated by the student or the teacher, can lead to emotional harm, abuse of power, manipulation, and, more often, criminal charges. Parents who partner with their children as their coaches will make efforts to be vigilant and identify possible behaviors in their students, their teachers, or the environment that might lend themselves to a potential point of entry that can be avoided or blocked.

WARNING SIGNS AND RED FLAGS OF INAPPROPRIATE RELATIONSHIPS

While there are no foolproof ways to know if such a relationship is being initiated, some of the relationships that have been found seem to have one or more of the following characteristics mentioned.

1. **Grooming behavior**: The individual may try to establish trust and build a relationship with a vulnerable person, using gifts, flattery, and manipulation to gain their trust and loyalty. This may involve physical contact that is unnecessary, unprovoked, or inappropriate.

2. **Secrecy**: The individual may insist on keeping the relationship a secret from others, especially from family and friends, to maintain control and prevent interference. Perhaps in this case, a parent may initiate general conversations about teachers and then ask about a specific teacher and there is a consistent desire not to discuss the teacher at all. This may not be a huge clue, but perhaps there is something there, especially if the student has

been commenting on other items about the teacher unrelated to academics, prior, i.e., personal appearance or attraction.

3. **Isolation**: The individual may try to isolate the student from their support network, creating a sense of dependence and making it harder for the student to seek intervention. When children are known to be introverts, lonely, or in isolation, some students are perceived as easy targets because it is believed that they are less likely to have a support system at home. It becomes ever so important that parents continue to make their students a part of their worlds, making soft and affirming eye contact often and initiating conversations regularly. All students need such companionship even if it is perceived that the student is too busy or not interested in your conversations. Students want to hear and be heard as they continue to evolve into adults. Parents, no matter how it looks, be that available support for them.

4. **Excessive jealousy**: The initiator or participant may display possessive and controlling behavior, becoming overly jealous and monitoring the other's activities and interactions. This may be observed even in casual conversation if it is present in your student. There is not likely a substantive reason for a student to be more protective of one teacher over another.

5. **Inappropriate boundaries**: The individual may push or ignore personal boundaries, crossing lines that make the person feel uncomfortable or unsafe. For example, a teacher and student may use their personal email addresses to communicate and not use the school-assigned email addresses. School emails generally have software installed that scan for implicit language and has the capability to archive email exchanges for later recall. Using a personal email instead of the school's monitored email, students and teachers can avoid the scrutiny of such monitoring systems.

SCHOOL PROTOCOLS AND PROTECTIONS

It is essential for students and teachers to maintain appropriate boundaries with students and adhere to professional codes of conduct to ensure a safe, fair and conducive learning environment. There are protections within the school system that are intended to avoid or make such relationships less likely to thrive.

SUGGESTIONS/RECOMMENDATIONS FOR CONSIDERATION

- **Parents - Start with your student.** By emphasizing the importance of setting and maintaining physical boundaries, parents clearly communicate to their students a belief in the ability to create and maintain safe spaces. Doing this by re-telling personal short stories or other true stories that I know helps me to have a varied way of delivering messages. There is absolutely no shortage of stories in the news about inappropriate student/teacher relationships and how such relationships develop so seemingly casual. We have all heard," I can tell you that the stove is hot so that you can avoid a bad decision, or you can hope to live through experiencing a bad decision to make a better decision the next time."

    Parents will also need to be prepared if these boundaries extend beyond the school building into the home or into the homes of people they trust. Unfortunately, involuntary, predatory, or inappropriate behaviors extended with a minor are not confined to one location. Though some reports suggest that relationships among students and teachers have consistently increased, inappropriate encounters with family members are sadly more often undetected. We usually view hugs or kisses, for instance, as a form of greeting, or maybe even placing a child on a lap as a typical practice; however, as a parent, being willing to support your child should either feel uncomfortable or should you decide that prior traditions should no longer be the norm.

- **Parents – Consider being "tech-vigilant."** Communications among teachers and students should be conducted on official school emails or software IF the school has them. Phone calls to and from teachers should be performed at a time that suggests professional exchange, except in the case of an emergency. This is non-negotiable for me. *Consistently* communicating on unofficial emails, on the phone during appropriate timeframes, or within the portal is a definite expectation.

- **Be Visual. Meet Your Students Teachers -** The discernment of a parent is unparalleled. Routinely meeting with teachers is essential for many reasons, especially academically, but being visible to a teacher will also allow the teacher to know that the student has a support system. It also communicates to other teachers that a parent would be receptive to knowing perceived sexual or romantic advances that their student is initiating. This trust is only present when other teachers have seen that a parent is a calm communicator and a caring advocate. **Note of warning** to the wise again: Parents must control their first reactions if erratic behavior or strong language is the first thought when advocating for their children. It is not always easy, but ultimately, doing so is the best practice. We need our children not only to graduate but to learn and have the best opportunities while in K12. Whether we believe so or not, this is harder when we make teachers our targets of frustration; Teachers can be (and most of the time are) our most available source of direction and assistance for our students. Finally, it can be a challenge for parents to accept that our student may be the aggressor, but being there as parents to guide them away from a poor decision may be an action that a student will appreciate later in life.

- **Inappropriate references:** Any verbal communication that is sexual, overly personal or secretive should be addressed. If there is an unusual fondness for a teacher, even if a student is not dismayed by the inappropriate relationship, reminding them of the legal implications for the other party (the legal adult) may be enough to discourage participation in an improper relationship.

- **Repor**t: If you believe an inappropriate relationship develops, remain calm and express your concern with the teacher or principal in a private setting (outside of the eyes of a classroom). After the conversation, if you are not assured that your suspicions are unfounded (even if they have been), you may want to send a "recap of conversation" email summarizing the discussion. Make the communications heartfelt and believe with high hopes that your assertion will redirect and plan for inappropriate behaviors. I always say hope but verify. In other words, continue to be vigilant. The school system also advocates for students to ensure they are doing what is possible to avoid such situations.

PROTECTIONS AND POLICIES WITHIN SCHOOLS

Schools have several policies that govern their existence that are intended to discourage inappropriate behaviors among students and staff. Some of the protocols and policy generalizations are as follows:

1. **Child Protection Laws**: Inappropriate relationships between adults and students are often in violation of child protection laws, which aim to safeguard the well-being and safety of minors. These laws vary by state but generally prohibit adults in positions of authority, such as teachers, from engaging in intimate relationships with students supported by federal law.

2. **Duty of Care**: School staff have what is referred to as a duty of care towards their students, which includes maintaining appropriate boundaries and ensuring a safe learning environment. Engaging in inappropriate relationships breaches the *duty of care* and can result in legal liability, such as certificate revocation or incarceration.

3. **Code of Conduct**: Most schools have Code of Conduct policies that outline the expected behavior of teachers, staff, and students. Engaging in inappropriate relationships violates this code and can

lead to disciplinary action, including termination of employment or potential jail time. This code is usually readily available on the school's website or can be requested by call or visit to the front office of the school

4. **Reporting Obligations**: Teachers and school staff members must often report any suspicions of abuse or misconduct to the appropriate authorities. Failure to report an inappropriate relationship can also have legal implications and may result in criminal charges or professional reputational loss. However, it is hard to say that every teacher will report an observation when so much of what is seen or observed may be subjective. Further, the mere fact of inferring or being accusatory without strong evidence can also be inflammatory. Parents should know again that romantic relationships are usually kept as secret as possible by those who participate in them and can be hidden for years.

In conclusion, engaging in inappropriate adult relationships within schools can have serious professional and legal consequences. All individuals in the education field need to maintain professional boundaries and uphold ethical standards to protect the well-being and safety of students. It is equally important that students not be the aggressor in pursuing romantic relationships with school staff. Yes, a minor is always to be protected, and adult teachers are expected to make appropriate decisions. Unfortunately, we know that both young and older people make poor choices at points in their lives. Even when students do not want to accept their responsibility for self-control or their responsibility to report inappropriate behavior, keeping them informed of suspicious behaviors may still be the appropriate choice.

Let's clear this up once and for all. Schools in the poorest neighborhoods are not the only institutions that are plagued with problems of drug use. The far-reaching effects of drugs on students both academically, emotionally, and physically are pervasive, from the richest to the poorest academic establishments. Get this fact embedded into your personal database of student knowledge. As parents, we hope that our children will never be tempted or even coerced into what can be a very dark world. Yet the data associated with drug use in K12 schools indicates that drug use is more prevalent than any of us would like it to be. In 2021, the Adolescent Behaviors and Experiences survey reported that 31.6% of high school students admitted that they had either used tobacco (vaping, cigarettes), alcohol, marijuana, or opioids in the last 30 days.[40] Opioids use has become highly known for its lethal use outcomes associated in even in the smallest amounts. Some Opioid awareness campaigns identify that even using the drug in amounts as small as what would fit on a pencil tip can result in death. In fact, the misuse and accidental overdose of Opioids in the student-age demographic is rapidly becoming the focus in the medical community.[41] Many states have started aggressive training plans to educate students and educators about the unknown dangers of using the drug.

There is no one way that some students are led to drugs. Students who grow up in a home where drug use is normal are thought to be even more likely to start and continue drug use in their own lives. In addition, peer pressure to be in the "cool" group can also be another driver. During the K12 years, it is not odd for a student to really want to fit in or be popular. Unfortunately, drug use can be a poor behavior that bonds students together in what is often considered a grownup behavior. In addition, the stress of high academic expectations can also drive students to seek stimulants that will keep them up longer and give them energy after having minimal sleep.[42] The impacts of these varied drugs have many similarities.

---

40   Hedgar, J., (2022).
41   McCabe et al., (2020).
42   McCabe et al., (2020).

IMPACT: THE POTENTIAL IMPACT OF DRUG USE ON ACADEMIC PERFORMANCE AND SOCIAL BEHAVIORS

Drug use can have a significant impact on academic performance and social behaviors. In terms of academic performance, drug use can impair cognitive function, memory, and concentration, making it difficult for students to focus and retain information. This inevitably results in poor academic performance, lower grades, difficulties in completing assignments, performing inadequately on exams and assessments, in worse cases, failed classes. Some studies support the belief that most brain growth and shaping of a child's brain functions are most actively growing from age 0—5; Given this belief, early drug use could potentially have even more severe and long-lasting consequences. If students do not function in complete awareness, they could quickly lose their enthusiasm for school because their academic efforts do not yield promising results.

Socially, drug use can negatively impact relationships with friends, family, and peers. It can lead to withdrawal from family activities, isolation, and decreased connection with others. Drug use can also contribute to increased conflicts and misunderstandings within social circles, as individuals may exhibit erratic behavior and mood swings.

Overall, the potential impact of drug use on individual growth, academic performance and social behaviors is troubling given the known prevalence of drug use in K12 settings. As a parent, many symptoms might help you to identify that there may be a potential opportunity to help your students to avoid the pitfalls associated with drug use. It can disrupt one's ability to succeed academically and maintain healthy relationships, ultimately affecting their overall well-being and future opportunities. It is important for individuals struggling with drug use to seek help and support in order to address these issues and make positive changes in their lives.

INTERVENTION: RECOGNIZING THE WARNING SIGNS AND SYMPTOMS OF DRUG USE IN CHILDREN AND TEENAGERS

Recognizing the warning signs and symptoms of drug use in children and teenagers is crucial for parents to intervene early and get their children the help they need. Here are some ways parents might recognize potential signs of drug use:

1. Changes in behavior: Parents should pay attention to sudden changes in their child's behavior, such as increased secrecy, mood swings, withdrawal from family and friends, and sudden aggressiveness or rebelliousness.

2. Physical symptoms: Identify physical symptoms that may indicate drug use, such as bloodshot eyes, dilated pupils, changes in appetite or sleep patterns, and sudden weight loss or gain.

3. Decline in academic performance: Parents should monitor their child's academic performance and look for any possible cause for signs of declining grades, skipped classes, or sudden disinterest in schoolwork.

4. Changes in social behavior: Parents should be aware of sudden changes in their child's social behavior, such as a new group of friends, increased isolation, or a loss of interest in previous hobbies or activities.

5. Drug paraphernalia: Keep an eye out for drug paraphernalia, such as pipes, needles, lighters, or small plastic bags that may indicate drug use.

PREVENTION: EXPLORING THE REASONS WHY STUDENTS MAY TURN TO DRUGS IN THE K12 SETTING

Outsmarting Peer Pressure: As students grow and socialize with their peers, they may be pressured to fit in or be accepted by a particular group. This pressure can lead students to experiment with drugs as a way to seek approval or feel included. Parents may want to consider routine checks and balances from time to time with their children to attempt to identify when other influence are at play and prior to having those influences become strongholds.

Stress and Academic Pressure: The demanding nature of schoolwork, exams, and extracurricular activities can create significant stress for students. In an attempt to cope with the pressure, some students may turn to drugs as a form of self-medication or escape from pressure.

Mental Health Issues: Students experiencing mental health issues such as anxiety, depression, or trauma may turn to drugs as a way to cope with their emotional distress. Loneliness can also result in severe depression. I believe now more than ever, students feel isolated. Parents sometimes work many hours to support the family, and schools are overpopulated. Teachers can be overwhelmed and far too tasked to see students as individuals. Though some students may not openly state that they desire closer family ties, there are some that I believe certainly long for such attachments. Drugs may provide temporary relief from their mental health symptoms, leading to a cycle of dependence.

Curiosity and Experimentation: Some students may be curious about the effects of drugs and may experiment with them out of interest or boredom. The desire to explore new experiences or sensations can drive students to try drugs without fully understanding the risks involved.

Influence of Media and Popular Culture: The glamorization of drug use in movies, music, and social media can influence students' perceptions and attitudes toward drugs. Exposure to such portrayals may normalize drug use and make it seem appealing or cool to some students.

Family Environment: Students who come from homes where drug use is prevalent or where there is a lack of parental supervision may be more likely to turn to drugs themselves. Remember children are great imitators of what they have seen even if what they have seen occurred at an age younger than many believe they were able to comprehend.

Lack of Proper Education and Awareness: In some cases, students may turn to drugs due to a lack of awareness about the potential risks and consequences associated with drug use. Without adequate education on drugs and their effects, students may be more susceptible to trying them without fully understanding the implications of use, even in small amounts.

SUGGESTIONS/RECOMMENDATIONS

Communications: Emphasize the importance of open communication. Encourage your child to come to you with any questions or concerns they may have about drugs. Let them know that you are there to support and guide them.

Be a positive role model: Children learn by example, so demonstrate healthy behaviors and decision-making in your own life. Show your child how to handle stress and difficult situations without turning to drugs.

Seek Educational Exposure: Provide accurate information about the risks and consequences of drug use. Share the facts about the effects of drugs on the body and brain. Libraries, schools, and Google Scholar are excellent sources of information. Use age-appropriate language: Tailor your language and explanations to your child's age and level of understanding. Keep the conversation simple and avoid using scare tactics. If you have experiences that have changed your life where drug use was involved or even occurrences of which you are aware to be truthful, sharing that information with your student will give them real-time information to store in their database maybe for later reference. Encourage questions and listen: Create a safe space for your child to ask questions and express their thoughts and concerns. Listen actively and address any misconceptions they may have. "Because I said so " may not be well received and will not serve as an educational reference that has a real foundation upon which to pull when independent decision-making is needed.

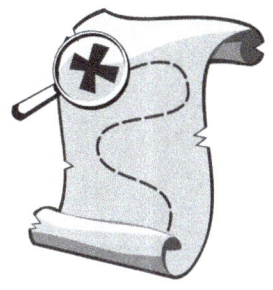

CHAPTER 11

BEYOND THE BELL SCHEDULE THE TREASURE WITHIN EXTRACURRICULAR ACTIVITIES

By participating in recreational activities, K12 students gain far more benefits than "playing." While physical activity is vital in the overall physical health of K12 students, recreation also offers several physical, social, and mental benefits. From organized sports to artistic interests, a wide variety of recreational activities are available to K12 students. Let us explore some of the more common activities available to students and highlight some possible benefits of stacking their social and academic toolboxes for future success. As parents, one of our goals is to give our children opportunities to make social and academic gains. It is important to note that there is more than one way to meet this objective. A parent might be genuinely concerned that their child is more of an introvert, inactive, unwilling to share, or a challenged communicator. The choices within extracurricular activities are vast and often offer more than the benefit of physical activity. Teaching socialization skills such as teamwork and critical thinking are among other associated benefits. Additionally, some colleges highly regard diverse backgrounds and interests, which can sometimes be demonstrated through academic transcripts that include school-based extracurricular activities.

FEW COMMON BENEFITS OF EXTRACURRICULAR ACTIVITIES

Cultivating leadership and self-confidence - Extracurricular activities expose students to leadership opportunities that are not always readily available in academic settings. Whether it's captaining a sports team, leading a debate club, capturing a first chair position in a band, or organizing a fundraiser, these activities require your minds to take charge and guide your peers toward a common goal. This hands-on experience allows students to develop essential leadership qualities like decision-making, problem-solving, effective communication, and teamwork. Students learn to inspire and motivate others, delegate tasks, and make effective use of everyone's skills and abilities. Such experiences help students build confidence in their own abilities.

Furthermore, participating in extracurricular activities helps students build their sense of self-confidence. By engaging in activities outside the classroom, students are exposed to new challenges and opportunities for personal growth. For example, joining a theater club allows students to step out of their comfort zones and perform in front of an audience. This experience boosts their self-esteem and confidence in their abilities. The support and encouragement from peers and mentors in extracurricular activities also boost self-confidence as students receive recognition for their achievements.

Interconnection and Community - Extracurricular activities foster a sense of belonging and interconnectedness within a community. Students actively participating in activities often feel a stronger connection to their school or organization. This sense of belonging increases self-confidence as students develop a support network of like-minded individuals with similar interests. Being a part of a community also encourages students to become more engaged and invested in their personal growth, which further contributes to their leadership development. More recently, there have been troubling reports that suggest that children are reporting feelings of isolation and loneliness. The suicide rate among students is also troubling. Involving students in communities of like-minded students in areas they enjoy will serve as a catalyst to reduce feelings of isolation as well.

Time Management and Order - Participation in extracurricular activities also nurtures skills that are transferable to other areas of life. For instance, time management skills are essential when balancing schoolwork, extracurricular activities, and personal commitments. Students who participate in such activities learn to prioritize and manage their time efficiently, which also helps them excel academically. These skills are not only beneficial during their school years but also in their future careers, where leadership qualities and self-confidence are highly valued.

Participation in extracurricular activities also nurtures skills that are transferable to other areas. For instance, time management skills are essential when balancing schoolwork, extracurricular activities, and personal commitments. Students who engage in such activities learn to prioritize and manage their time better, which helps them excel academically. These skills are not only beneficial during their school years but also in their future careers, where leadership qualities and self-confidence are highly valued.

Students learn that repetitive activities or practices produce desirable results. For example, while participating in a sport and being coached by a coach, students quickly learn the emphasis a coach places on repeatedly performing an activity that leads to mastery through practice. This learning could positively impact a student's perceived importance for setting aside time for homework and expecting a desired result.

SPOTLIGHT ON SPECIFIC EXTRACURRICULAR ACTIVITIES AND BENEFITS

Some of the activities listed below were selected because they are considered more commonplace. In contrast, others were included because of the vast projection of their impact or perceived influence in years to come. Disclaimer: For every good research result found, there could be bad associated. These are suggestions of benefits for your toolkit consideration that might benefit your student, and before they realize it, YOU, the involved parent, have enhanced their overall being. (Blink Blink). They will thank you later!

1. **Sports**: Sports activities such as soccer, basketball, baseball, tennis, lacrosse, swimming, track and field hockey are not only great for physical fitness but also teach valuable life skills such as *teamwork*, *discipline*, and *perseverance*. I enjoyed watching their innocence while participating in sports. I never saw any fights or open disagreements about **race, ethnicity, or class. The students** quickly recognized the gifts in each other, respected each other's gifts, and worked in harmony to win! They laughed together when they won and tried to fight back tears when they lost. Many schools offer intramural sports teams and after-school sports programs where students can actively participate and compete.

2. **Performing Arts**: Activities like drama, dance, music, and theater allow students to express themselves *creatively*. These activities help improve *self-confidence, public* **speaking skills, and teamwork**. School bands, choirs, orchestras, and drama clubs often organize performances, allowing students to display their talents and further build confidence in young adults. Activities such as marching band also couple the benefits of physical activity with the discipline needed.

3. **Arts and Crafts**: Painting, pottery, sculpture, and other art forms provide an outlet for creativity and self-expression. These

activities enhance artistic skills and foster **patience, focus, and attention to detail**. Schools often organize art clubs or classes where students can explore their artistic interests. Students who may be less likely to express themselves verbally may choose to do so through their art as an outlet to communicate their needs and their likes or dislikes.

4. **Community Service (Volunteer)**: Engaging in community service activities helps students develop a sense of empathy, compassion, and community connectedness. Volunteer opportunities at facilities such as local homeless shelters or food banks allow students to contribute to improvements in their communities and learn worthwhile life lessons.

5. **Technology, Esports, Chess, and Coding**: In today's digital age, activities like coding, robotics, and esports have become increasingly popular, and for good reason. Esports are projected to grow even faster than traditional sports in popularity and associated economic wealth.[43] These activities teach students to develop problem-solving and critical thinking skills while learning about fields that are projected to hold most of the growth and job opportunities for the future. Schools often incorporate technology-focused clubs or classes to introduce students to these important subjects. For instance, Esports are projected to grow even faster than traditional sports in popularity and associated economic wealth. Also, do not overlook the growing number of colleges that offer Esports as a major or offer scholarships for Esports; As of 2018, there were approximately 200 colleges offering Esports.[44] The two definitions most associated with these extracurricular activities in schools are Science, Technology, Engineering, and Math (STEM) or Science, Technology, Engineering, Arts, and Math (STEAM). Please note that the acronyms STEM and STEAM are more commonly heard.

---

43   Trotter et al., (2022).
44   Heilweil, (2019).

When my son was in middle school, one of the extracurricular activities "I" wanted him to like was chess because of all I had read about the sports scholarship. Also, I strongly believed that my son needed to be challenged to keep his attention. The school and recreation centers he attended did not offer chess, so I searched the internet and found a private school in the area, St. Christopher's School, that offered a class in the summer for a few weeks. Initially, he was excited because the instructor was a known chess champion. He played for a bit and defeated a few family members and friends, to their dismay! The beauty of this experience was two-fold. One, my son had an opportunity to be exposed to something new. Secondly, he had an additional opportunity to interact with children from private schools of various cultures and racial backgrounds. He could see what I saw in him, and that was that his hard work, though in a public school, would allow him to be comfortable in any setting he chose to enter.

6. **Mind and Body**: Practices such as meditation have become more popular among adults, so more students will likely practice these concentration processes to improve their perceived ***stress relief*** qualities. Schools can offer mindfulness sessions or facilitate meditation clubs to support students' mental health. A child's home surroundings may be more complicated than quiet. Such activities may be a great benefit for students to reduce stress and promote clarity.

As this chapter closes, YES, there must be a tremendous acknowledgement of the time requirement from parents to get students to and from activities that are after school in some cases. As a single mother, running from basketball to soccer and soccer to football was often a stretch, for instance. There were just a few parents I trusted along the way to pick up while I dropped off sometimes or vice versa. This partnership with other parents (and for me it was a small number of parents I cherish and trust to this day) helped my son obtain some of the benefits of these activities. I do not regret one moment invested and believe in the powerful value of extracurricular activities.

CHAPTER 12

THE GIFT OF LIKE MINDS GIFTED AND TALENTED STUDENT COMMUNITIES

I must admit this in full transparency: When I was in high school, I took a *few* advanced classes. I must be honest and emphasize a few. When my son approached middle school, I had to revisit the value of class types with him. I needed to *reintroduce* myself first and then introduce him to the pros and cons of various class types (Dual enrollment, Advanced Placement, and Gifted and Talented). These class types are beyond the general course offerings in high school.

To refamiliarize myself, I begin by diving into the definitions of these three types of programs. As a baseline of understanding, these are not a set of three specific classes but a classification of classes in which some courses are associated. There are advantages and disadvantages to all the programs. One advantage to all these programs usually is that class sizes are smaller and may allow for more teacher-student interaction, but there are particular characteristics associated with each program.

ADVANCED PLACEMENT (AP)

Advanced Placement classes are slightly higher-level classes usually taken on the high school campus. Do not be dismayed; students do not have to be potential physicists to thrive in these classes. Students in AP classes usually possess good study habits and take pride in their achievements.

PROS

- These classes usually award more credits than other classes and can potentially **reduce the time required for a student to meet the minimum high school graduation requirements**. For instance, instead of a class awarding three credits, AP classes may award four or five credits per class.
- **Higher Overall GPA** - Since these classes have more weighted credits, this can positively increase a student's grade point average (GPA) compared to other students. The result is an AP student enrolled in the same number of high school classes as another student *not* taking AP classes will potentially have a higher GPA at the end of the school year. Thus, an AP student may be awarded more class superlatives and be viewed more positively by colleges than other students because of a higher GPA. In short, AP class completion can be attractive to colleges because participation proves that a student will likely succeed at college.
- **Some colleges accept AP classes in their curriculums**. With a bit of research, a student can find out which schools will accept the AP classes that might be taken in their high school. The high school counselor is a great resource to consult to learn what arrangements might have been made to accept the school's AP classes into local colleges.
- Passing an AP test and obtaining credits for the class **does NOT require a student to take a class**. Students can schedule to take a standardized AP subject test at a small cost, and when the

student passes, the student is awarded credits. This is a win for two reasons (if not more):

#1 The student could potentially take these freshman-level course tests before entering a college during high school and earn college credits.

#2 A student (a family) can save thousands of dollars by taking and passing AP tests that will satisfy some of the college courses required for a nominal cost compared to the actual class cost.

- The rigor of some high school classes is thought to be stagnant due, in part, to the overall reality that many students fell behind by grade levels during the global pandemic shutdown.[45] Some college students later complain of being ill-prepared for college. In fact, many freshman college students do not meet the minimum requirements for mathematics when entering college and find themselves taking remedial classes in college to get on track for their selected college programs.[46] Taking AP Mathematics and English courses in high school could ensure a student is **better prepared for college-level courses.**

CONS:

- These classes, like general classes, have a grade awarded at the end of the semester; however, ***there can be an additional AP test requirement*** at the end of the course to demonstrate the student's level of subject mastery.
- Some ***colleges may not accept the AP classes taken in high school*** into their curriculum. Researching some of the colleges where a student will apply will reveal a more definitive and personalized answer.

---

45   Dorn et al., (2021).
46   Bailey et al., (2005); Epper and Baker, (2009).

DUAL ENROLLMENT

Most schools will require that a student be approved to participate in this program. If offered by a high school, students can enroll in college-level freshman and sophomore classes, usually in grades 11 and 12.

PROS:

▪ One of the biggest pros is that students can earn college credits for free! In this program, students can be very close to earning an associate's degree before leaving high school. What a win in many ways. First, parents nor students pay one penny of a monetary investment for the college courses taken in high school. The school pays for these college-level courses!! This is undoubtedly a way for parents to save money that would have otherwise been needed for college.

▪ Students can become acquainted with the rigor and lifestyle associated with college lifestyles while in high school and learn to adjust their character or study practices before transitioning to the "paid" arena of college. Some students can become overwhelmed by the requirement differences in college when taking a full load of classes (5 or more classes) in college. Dual enrollment allows students to take 1-2 college-level courses in high school, which permits reduced exposure to the time and focus requirement while preparing high school students for the college lifestyle to come.

▪ **Live exposure to the college lifestyle.** High school dual enrollment courses are sometimes held on college campuses. Some high schools offer transportation to the college or pay for transportation. If a student has never been on a college campus, they will be in classrooms with actual college freshmen and sophomores. The class is not generally confined to dual enrollment, so students receive direct exposure to college culture. A high school student may have four classes at their normal high school, and their 5th class is at the local college campus. Schools have planned to avoid all the time restrictions to ensure high-school students have ample time to reach their college campus for one or two classes of the day or week.

CONS:

Enrollment in these classes may be limited depending upon the school district and its affiliation with local colleges. In some cases, the district for the high school is paying for these classes, so offering these classes may be a sizable investment within the school budget or funding sources. In other cases, the state or a grant may fund the investment of early college classes. This means that the student and parent should seek information before or during freshman year to learn what would make them more attractive to being accepted into the program if participation is the goal. Perhaps try to identify the lead person for the program early as a strategic action towards learning more and providing your students exposure. For instance, this person may also teach freshman or sophomore classes. Being in their class prior to selection time or introducing yourself and knowing that they influence program acceptance later is a good piece of information to consider as your student put their best foot forward to show their interest and readiness.

- **Participation will require a higher level of effort**. This can be negative or positive. College-level classes in freshman year can be very similar to intense high-school courses. The students admitted into these programs have often demonstrated in 9th and 10th-grade years that they are focused studiers and have consistently earned grades mostly in the A-B range. It's important to note that an occasional C earned does not necessarily exclude students from program qualification; however, the acceptance criteria will be specific to each school's participation in such programs.
- **Credit Acceptance into college programs can vary.** School districts that participate in Dual Enrollment programs generally

meet with colleges to identify classes available for high school students that will later be accepted into their college curriculums. Often, the dual-enrollment classes are general 101 classes in English, Math, or Science offered by colleges. Many of these freshman-level classes are accepted in various colleges. Still, if a high school student has early acceptance into a college or is targeting a college, it may be prudent to make very certain that the high-school classes taken in dual enrollment will be transferable to the college of their choice.

GIFTED AND TALENTED

The classes usually encourage and attract more creativity and participation from students. Growing in independence and fueling a love for science, technology, engineering and mathematics can also be at the core for these classes.

PROS:

- Students generally build **stronger self-confidence** through communication and gain value associated with group collaboration.
- These classes can also be associated with **higher credit awards,** giving students a higher grade point average at the end of the high school year.
- College acceptance can be advantageous when college's view and compare student transcripts.
- Creative students have an opportunity to interact with like-minded students. Students can find their own feelings of belonging with other students who value the education process. Being around students who have positive values can invoke positive influences on different students to possess the same traits.
- **Supporting your child's social and emotional growth.** Gifted and talented students may have unique social and emotional needs that parents should be aware of and support, such as possible

perfectionism, peer relationships that may not exist in other settings, and stress management.

CONS:

- Programs *may not award college credits*.
- There may be **limited college cost savings**. Students may miss an opportunity to reduce costs associated with college if not associated with AP or Dual enrollment. If savings is a parent's goal, this may not be the desired path. Not many parents don't have the goal of saving money for college on the top of their minds!

As a note for either pro or con for all programs – these programs can have high requirements or not depending on the school. Parents, please review the requirements with your students, and if your student is experiencing more stress than is thought to be acceptable in a class, next semester, you will want to consider the possibility of returning to a class schedule that may be less demanding.

FINAL SUMMARY (TIPS):

Parents need to be aware that acceptance into all these classes may be competitive, and the seats in the classrooms are limited. Explore what the requirements are to be considered for these classes. Have your student secure information on the requirements from the school, likely the counselor. No matter how interested or intelligent your child is (and remember, your student does not have to be an advanced scholar to be accepted), do NOT wait for your student to be asked to participate in these classes. If you believe these are a good fit for your student, find out the criteria, make sure your student meets them, and ASK to be invited to class participation early. That means in freshman year, families should make the effort to find out what is required to be enrolled in these classes and who decides on who attends and who does not. Is everyone who expresses interest and meets the qualifications admitted? If not, what makes the selected students stand out in the selection process? I want to stress that admittance can be competitive, and it's not always the smartest students in the room but the students who have a parent who asks questions and requests their child's participation.

As always, this chapter ends with a gentle reminder that numerous student advocates exist in schools. Many teachers and administrators are in schools because they are gifted to help students. By being courteous, asking questions, and displaying professionally (calmly but straightforward) that you want to ensure your student has access to these classes, parents progress in a path that often yields the desired results. Building positive and collaborative relationships with your student's teachers and school staff can help ensure they receive the support and enrichment they need in these specialized classes. Parents can play a crucial role in advocating for their child's placement when prepared with the class acceptance criteria (often found on the school website as well) and a gentle exhibit (a phone call to the counselor or principal inquiring about participation early) that their child has a visual advocate.

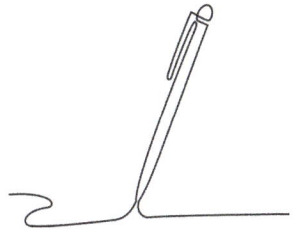

A FINAL THOUGHT

Bridges are most often manmade structures. At times we can see in the distance what awaits us, our destinations, prior to our actual arrival. Other times, we only believe that the bridge we are approaching will lead us to a desirable place because others have traveled the same course.

Parents and school districts are the bridges for this generation's students. Though some adults might say "they themselves overcame obstacles," I, at my core, believe that students need our help to avoid the stress and trauma of this era. I know this is easily suggested, but even working multiple jobs, parents must find a way to make certain their children feel safe, secure, and loved. A part of that love is to help them navigate waters **now** that could threaten their quality of life later. Active participation in obtaining education still has an impact on the future. Being a partner to your children, parents help children strategically plan and encourage them that winning academically is possible. Do not discount your value because you do not know algebra! You are a mentor or coach for your children, and your wisdom and belief in their ability to prosper in education carry much weight. Don't give up on them, ever. Supportively push them, no matter what your past, your background, or your education may be. They will not forget your example to openly love and support them in such a meaningful way.

From one K12 coach to another - All Things Are Possible When You Believe in Children Without Ceasing.

All the Best,
Dr. Cassandra Harris

BIBLIOGRAPHY

- Adelman, C. *The Toolbox Revisited: Paths to Degree Completion from High School Through College.* Washington, DC: U.S. Department of Education, 2006.

- Altonji, J. G. "The Effects of High School Curriculum on Education and Labor Market Outcomes." *The Journal of Human Resources* 30, no. 3 (1995): 409-438.

- Bailey, T., Jenkins, D., and Leinbach, T. *Community College Low-Income and Minority Student Completion Study: Descriptive Statistics from the 1992 High School Cohort.* New York, NY: Teachers College, Columbia, 2005.

- Bell, Larry I. *12 Powerful Words.* Manassas, VA: Multicultural America, 2005.

- Bogenschneider, K. "Parental Involvement in Adolescent Schooling: A Proximal Process with Transcontextual Validity." *Journal of Marriage and the Family* 59, no. 3 (1997): 718–33.

- Bryson, Anna. "State Data Shows Ongoing Teacher Shortage in Virginia." January 6, 2024. *Richmond.com.*

- *Cambridge Dictionary.* Accessed August 15, 2024. https://dictionary.cambridge.org/dictionary/english/.

- "Can Food Insecurity Affect Cognitive Performance of School Children." *International Journal of Psychology and Behavioral Sciences* 11, no. 3 (2021): 41–46. https://doi.org/10.5923/j.ijpbs.20211103.01.

- Chamorro, Maria. "Can We Explain Students' Failure in Learning Multiplication?" In *Handbook of Mathematics Education,* edited by Jane Smith, 201–217. New York: Routledge, 2021.

- Chang, H. N., and M. Romero. *Present, Engaged, and Accounted For: The Critical Importance of Addressing Chronic Absence in the Early Grades.* New York, NY: National Center for Children in Poverty, 2008.

- Cheung, C. S-S., and E. M. Pomerantz. "Why Does Parents' Involvement Enhance Children's Achievement? The Role of Parent-Oriented Motivation." *Journal of Educational Psychology* 104, no. 3 (2012): 820. https://doi.org/10.1037/a0027183.

- *Chronic Absenteeism in the Nation's Schools.* Accessed August 25, 2024. https://ed.gov.

- Clements, D. H., and J. Sarama. *Learning and Teaching Early Math: The Learning Trajectories Approach.* New York, NY: Routledge, 2009.

- Coleman-Jensen, A., Rabbitt, M., Gregory, C., and Singh, A. "Household Food Security in the United States in 2019." *ERR-256.* Washington, DC: U.S. Department of Agriculture, Economic Research Service, 2019.

- Congress.gov. "S.97 – Children's Internet Protection Act." Accessed August 25, 2024. https://www.congress.gov/bill/106th-congress/senate-bill/97/text.

- *Consumer Guide: Children's Internet Protection Act (CIPA).* Accessed July 5, 2024. https://www.fcc.gov/sites/default/files/childrens_internet_protection_act_cipa.pdf.

- Cratty, Dorothyjean. "Do 3rd Grade Math Scores Determine Students' Futures? A Statewide Analysis of College Readiness and the Income Achievement Gap." August 11, 2014. *SSRN*. https://ssrn.com/abstract=2442671.

- Dorn, E., Hancock, B., Sarakatsannis, J., and Viruleg, E. *COVID-19 and Education: The Lingering Effects of Unfinished Learning.* McKinsey & Company, 2021.

- New America Media. "The Power of Parents: Research Underscores the Impact of Parent Involvement in Schools." *EdSource,* February 2014.

- *Education Commission of the States.* "50-State Comparison: State K-3 Policies." June 2, 2023. https://www.ecs.org/50-state-comparison-state-k-3-policies-2023/#:~:text=17%20states%20and%20the%20District,at%20least%20half%2Dday%20kindergarten.

- Ellwood-Lowe, Monica E., Foushee, Ruth, and Srinivasan, Mahesh. "What Causes the Word Gap? Financial Concerns May Systematically Suppress Child-Directed Speech." January 17, 2020. https://doi.org/10.31234/osf.io/byp4k.

- Epper, R., and Baker, E. *Technology Solutions for Developmental Mathematics: An Overview of Current and Emerging Practices.* Denver, CO: William & Flora Hewlett Foundation, Bill & Melinda Gates Foundation, 2009.

- Epstein, Joyce L., and Van Voorhis, Francis L. "More Than Minutes: Teachers' Roles in Designing Homework." *Educational Psychologist* 36, no. 3 (2001): 181–93. https://doi.org/10.1207/S15326985EP3603_4.

- Finn, Jeremy D. "Withdrawing from School." *Review of Educational Research* 59, no. 2 (1989): 117–42. https://doi.org/10.3102/00346543059002117.

- Fischer, Adrienne, Carlos Jamieson, Gerardo Silva-Padron, Lauren Peisach, Matt Weyer, Duncan, Greg J., Chantelle J. Dowsett, Amy

Claessens, Katherine Magnuson, Aletha C. Huston, Pamela Klebanov, Linda S. Pagani, Leon Feinstein, Mimi Engel, Jeanne Brooks-Gunn, Holly Sexton, Kathryn Duckworth, and Crista Japel. "School Readiness and Later Achievement." *Developmental Psychology* 43, no. 6 (2007): 1428–44.

- Gershenson, S., Jacknowitz, A., and Brannegan, A. "Are Student Absences Worth the Worry in U.S. Primary Schools?" *Education Finance and Policy* 12, no. 2 (2017): 137–65.

- Greenwood, C., Carta, J., Walker, D., Watson-Thompson, J., Schnitz, A., Thompson, V., Gabriel, D., Schneeberger, S., and Wallisch, A. *Bridging the Word Gap Research Network: Community Action Planning Guide.* University of Kansas, 2020. https://communityhealth.ku.edu/sites/communityhealth/files/files/BWG%20Community%20Action%20Planning%20Guide.pdf.

- Grolnick, Wendy, and Slowiaczek, Maria. "Parents' Involvement in Children's Schooling: A Multidimensional Conceptualization and Motivational Model." *Child Development* 65, no. 1 (1994): 237–52. https://doi.org/10.2307/1131378.

- Heckman, J. J., Stixrud, J., and Urzua, S. "The Effects of Cognitive and Noncognitive Abilities on Labor Market Outcomes and Social Behavior." *Journal of Labor Economics* 24, no. 3 (2006): 411–82.

- Hedgar, J. "Supporting School Efforts to Combat Drug Abuse." *National Association of State Board of Education,* vol. 29, no. 11 (2022).

- Heilweil, Rebecca. "College Esports Players Are Cashing in Big." *Wired,* 2019. https://www.wired.com/story/infoporn-college-esports-players-cashing-in-big/.

- Henderson, A. T., and Berla, A. *A New Generation of Evidence: The Family Is Critical to Student Achievement.* Washington, DC: National Committee for Citizens in Education, 1997.

- Kirksey, J. "Academic Harms of Missing High School and the Accuracy of Current Policy Thresholds: Analysis of Preregistered Administrative Data from a California School District." *AERA Open* 8 (2019): Article 23328584211071115.

- Korpershoek, H., Canrinus, E. T., Fokkens-Bruinsma, M., and de Boer, H. "The Relationship Between School Belonging and Students' Motivational, Social-Emotional, Behavioral, and Academic Outcomes in Secondary Education: A Meta-Analytic Review." *Research Papers in Education* 35, no. 6 (2020): 641–80. https://doi.org/10.1080/02671522.2019.1615116.

- Lenroot, R. K., and Giedd, J. N. "Brain Development in Children and Adolescents: Insights from Anatomical Magnetic Resonance Imaging." *Neuroscience and Biobehavioral Reviews* 30, no. 6 (2006): 718–29.

- Maleki, M., Chehrzad, M. M., Kazemnezhad Leyli, E., Mardani, A., and Vaismoradi, M. "Social Skills in Preschool Children from Teachers' Perspectives." *Children* 6 (2019): 64. https://doi.org/10.3390/children6020064.

- *NAEP Long-Term Trend Assessment Results: Reading and Mathematics.* Accessed 2022. https://www.nationsreportcard.gov/highlights/ltt/2022/#section-recent-student-performance-trends.

- National Center for Education Statistics. *English Learners in Public Schools. Condition of Education.* U.S. Department of Education, Institute of Education Sciences, 2024. Accessed [date]. https://nces.ed.gov/programs/coe/indicator/cgf.

- National Center for Education Statistics. *Nation's Report Card. National Assessment of Educational Progress.* Washington, DC: U.S. Department of Education, Institute of Education Sciences, 2019.

- National Center for Education Statistics. *Revenues and Expenditures for Public Elementary and Secondary Education: School Year 2021–22*

(Fiscal Year 2022). Washington, DC: U.S. Department of Education, Institute of Education Sciences, 2024. Accessed December 13, 2024. https://nces.ed.gov/pubs2024/2024301.pdf.

- National Center for Education Statistics. "Press Release, December 6, 2022." Accessed [date]. https://nces.ed.gov/whatsnew/press_releases/12_6_2022.asp.

- National Children's Advocacy Center. *Educator Sexual Misconduct: A Bibliography.* Huntsville, AL: Author, 2022.

- Ready, Douglas. D. "Socioeconomic Disadvantage, School Attendance, and Early Cognitive Development." *Sociology of Education* 83, no. 4 (2010): 271–86. https://doi.org/10.1177/0038040710383520.

- Rocque, Michael, Jennings, Wesley. G., Piquero, Alex R., Ozkan, Turgut, and Farrington, David P. "The Importance of School Attendance: Findings from the Cambridge Study in Delinquent Development on the Life-Course Effects of Truancy." *Crime and Delinquency* 63, no. 5 (2017): 592–612. https://doi.org/10.1177/0011128716660520.

- Sheldon, S. B. *School, Family, and Community Partnerships: Your Handbook for Action.* 3rd ed. USA: Corwin Press, 2009.

- Tan, Tiffany. S., Arellano, Ivett, and Patrick, Susan. Kemper. "State Teacher Shortages 2024 Update: Teaching Positions Left Vacant or Filled by Teachers Without Full Certification." *Learning Policy Institute,* 2024. https://learningpolicyinstitute.org/product/state-teacher-shortages-vacancy-2024.

- Trotter, Michael. G., Tristan J. Coulter, Paul A. Davis, Dylan R. Poulus, and Remco Polman. "Examining the Impact of School Esport Program Participation on Student Health and Psychological Development." *Frontiers in Psychology,* January 24, 2022.

- U.S. Department of Education. *Chronic Absenteeism in the Nation's Schools: An Unprecedented Look at a Hidden Educational Crisis.* 2016. https://www2.ed.gov/datastory/chronicabsenteeism.html.

- U.S. Department of Education. *Protecting Student Privacy: A Parent's Guide to the Family Educational Rights and Privacy Act (FERPA).* Accessed [date]. https://studentprivacy.ed.gov/sites/default/files/resource_document/file/A%20parent%20guide%20to%20ferpa_508.pdf.

- U.S. Census. "National Single Parent Day: March 21, 2024." Accessed [date]. https://www.census.gov/library/stories/2023/06/more-than-a-quarter-all-households-have-one-person.html#:~:text=The%20Current%20Population%20Survey%20(CPS,to%201.5M%20in%201950.

- White, Cornelious. "Learner-Centered Teacher-Student Relationships Are Effective: A Meta-Analysis." *Review of Educational Research* 77, no. 1 (2007): 113–43.

www.ingramcontent.com/pod-product-compliance
Lightning Source LLC
Chambersburg PA
CBHW071759120626
46550CB00002B/848